PERSONAL
FREEDOM

How The Gospel Can Be Good For Your Mental Health

Ken Yeow

BY HIS GRACE,

FOR HIS GLORY

Contents

ACKNOWLEDGEMENTS

With much appreciation to my wife, Yiing, whose love and care for me is unquestioned and provides a foundation for all I do.

Sincere thanks to the following who provided very helpful feedback on draft manuscripts: Steve Critchlow, Helen Douglas, Andy Heron, Brian Johnston, Werner McIlwaine, Joanne McKinstry, Pete O'Halloran, Michael Harrison, Gareth Patterson and Lalitha Velautham.

Eternal gratitude to Jesus Christ, Saviour and Lord, the true source of freedom.

Chapter 1

INTRODUCTION

Vision

Rom. 1:16:

> *For I am not ashamed of the gospel of Christ, for it is the power of God to salvation for everyone who believes, for the Jew first and also for the Greek.*

The aim of this book is to try and show how the gospel of Jesus Christ, properly understood and embraced, can potentially have a positive impact on a believer's mental health

---

It is my hope and prayer that as you read this book, the gospel will come alive to you in ways that are fresh and powerful, that you may know the transforming reality of God in all aspects of your being. It is my desire that those who are genuinely struggling in different areas of life will be helped to move from brokenness to maturity in the power of Christ, all for His glory.

A world in need

The world can be a very stressful place. Watch the news on any given day and you are likely to be bombarded by a litany of negative reports: political turmoil, economic crisis, natural disasters, horrific crimes, personal tragedies, the list goes on. Whilst remarkable advances in electronic technology have brought significant benefits, they have also contributed to a frantic pace of life and a paradoxical disconnection of relationships (I often wonder if we are losing the art of face-to-face conversation in this era of globe-spanning social media). National televised talents shows, personal growth and development seminars and even the image projected by some high profile church leaders[1] can create expectations of success which do not match the limitations of a person's reality.

Add to that the normal stresses and strains of everyday existence that markedly affect us internally: living with the shackles of past trauma, feelings of not/never measuring up, interpersonal conflicts of all sorts, intense pressure in the workplace, a daily struggle to make ends meet etc. and the burdens mount.

On top of this, for Christians, this is all happening within the context of an apparently burgeoning worldview that actively attacks faith in God, which is being labelled as irrational, irrelevant and even insidious. In this environment, for a believer who is not well-grounded in truth, the very foundations of what they say they stand for can be seriously shaken.

Often, more than we realise, behind the veneer of achievement and seemingly having it all together, a different personal story lies underneath. People are wounded, exhausted, confused, lost, anxious, depressed, despairing.

A common estimate is that one in four British adults will experience at least one diagnosable mental health problem in any given year[2]; around 6000 people – almost one every 90 minutes – took their own lives in the UK in 2012[3].

Where can the hurting find healing, direction and hope?

Christianity can provide real answers

The need to address significant personal difficulties has of course not gone unnoticed by the human endeavour. There is a proliferation of approaches claiming to help people solve their problems and feel better about them. The medical specialty of psychiatry and behavioural science of psychology are well-established fields of empirical research and clinical practice. Walk into any high street bookshop and you will likely find a well-stocked section on self-help/popular psychology, with titles of that genre having a consistent presence on bestseller lists.

Amidst the multitude of messages out there, this is an attempt to bring us back to age-old wisdom as it applies to modern day life. I seek to present eternal truths and their applications that can help us experience real personal freedom, so that we are able to live with true inner peace, joy and purpose.

The Bible can speak powerfully to all the key areas of life: physical, psychological, social as well as spiritual. This is not in the sense of it being a handy encyclopaedia or cookbook where a systematic collection of factual information or a step-by-step recipe can be pulled out to address every issue that human beings face. Rather, the Word of God shows us how we can enter into a life-giving relationship with the One who is the source of all wisdom, knowledge and understanding and that from this intimate union with Him, holistic positive transformation can become a reality.

In a sense, I am hoping that the core material here in terms of explaining the gospel in more detail will be 'nothing new' but will lead people to behold the good news of Jesus with fresh perspective and awe-inspired gratitude as the relevant applications of truth are made to the common struggles of everyday life.

Throughout these pages, I want to assist Christians to see what a great treasure they have in the gospel! I want believers to comprehend in greater breadth and depth what God has done and is doing for them and this world through the person of Jesus Christ and the power of His Holy Spirit. It would truly delight me to be able to boost, in the hearts of ordinary followers of Christ, a conviction regarding the sufficiency of Scripture for life in this complex contemporary age.

It is my earnest desire that people will find what they are really looking for in the grace and truth that can be found in Jesus. My hope is that any learning from this book will move them from the theoretical to the experiential, when actual godly change gradually and visibly occurs in the lives of faithful individuals (and subsequently whole communities of believers) to the point where the reality of God is clearly displayed to those who as yet do not know Him, and that He will be ultimately glorified.

An important point to note before progressing further: whilst this book is about how the gospel can potentially help people experience a greater degree of mental health, the main exhortation is that the gospel is to be believed and lived out because it is true and is God's plan for mankind, rather than because of the benefits it can lead to. This can be difficult to grasp in a consumer-driven, needs-led, psychologised culture where self enlightenment and satisfaction are dominant motivations.

To put it another way, the potential positive impact on a person's psychological and emotional wellbeing whenever they personally encounter the powerful truths of the gospel is a blessed by-product of belief in and experience of the truth itself, the person of Jesus Christ Himself. Rather than seeking the blessings first, we make core truth the primary aim and when we find this, manifold blessings ensue.

What do I mean by 'the gospel'?

A step-by-step explanation

The gospel (or, translated from its Greek root word, the 'good news') is the central message of the Christian faith, as revealed throughout the pages of the Bible. It is the story of God's redemptive plan for a fallen creation[4], achieved through the life, death and resurrection of His Son, Jesus Christ. It is the means by which sinful human beings can be forgiven and reconciled with a holy God, and a decaying universe be restored, recreated and reach its glorious destiny.

In its entirety, the gospel presents an illuminating understanding of the place of mankind within the world and helps to answer the big questions of life centred around:

- Meaning – 'Where did I come from?'; 'Who am I?'; 'What is the purpose of my life?'
- Morality – 'How should I live?'; 'How can I be good enough?' and
- Mortality – 'What happens when I die?'

For the purpose of this book, I have broken down the gospel as I understand it into 6 component parts (which is of course not the only way to do it). This is by no means to suggest that the gospel is simply a sequence of compartmentalised information; it is rather a flowing and coherent narrative that needs to be apprehended and experienced in all its fullness.

Nevertheless, it may be useful to consider separately, like facets of a sparkling jewel, the vital aspects of the gospel that come together to form the whole magnificent picture:

1) <u>It's all about Him</u>

God reveals Himself through His Word as a great God who is good and loving as well as holy and just, and who has created us to know Him. We need to come to terms with the fact that He is at the centre of the universe, not us, and that He is to be the object of all worship and trust now and forevermore. He is actively working out His plans and purposes for His creation, steadily bringing all things to a preordained majestic consummation.

2) The gift of brokenness

The reality of this life is that we live in a broken world where God's perfect design has been marred by wilful disobedience and rebellion at both celestial and human levels. Sin, the natural bent of human beings to function outside of submission to God, has become a pervasive, transgenerational malady. God in His grace allows us to encounter our own brokenness in order that we may turn to Him for salvation[5].

3) What Jesus has done

Through the death of Jesus Christ on our behalf and the provision of His righteousness as a gift of grace, we can through repentance and faith be made right with God; the theological term for this is justification, which brings freedom from the penalty of sin. We are subsequently adopted into the family of God, the church universal. The forgiveness of God provides an ultimate basis for Christians to walk in continual forgiveness and, where possible, interpersonal reconciliation.

4) Power to change

As we become believers in Jesus, the Holy Spirit comes to live within and empowers us to become more and more like Him. We are called to a new holiness and given the ability to pursue this in practice. Upon conversion to Christ, we enter into real spiritual conflict with the enemies of our soul: the devil and his cohorts, our uncrucified sinful nature and a world system antagonistic to the things of God. The process of growing in God by the enabling of the Holy Spirit is called sanctification, which is bringing freedom from the power of sin.

5) Eternal perspective

As followers of Christ, we live in the knowledge that this world is passing away and is but a herald of a better reality to come. God sustains us in the midst of the unavoidable trials and tribulations of this present existence. He is preparing us to rule and reign with Him in the new heavens and earth for all eternity. We can look forward with great hope to the future culmination of God's purposes for His creation i.e. glorification, which will bring freedom from the very presence of sin.

6) <u>Our response</u>

An ongoing response of repentance, faith, surrender and obedience is required in order to make the truths of the gospel applicable and personal in an individual believer's life throughout their spiritual journey; we have divine help with this. God Himself also supplies the grace for us to cultivate a devotional life that enables us to consistently live in the overcoming presence and power of His Spirit. Our response includes a life of outward-focused, selfless service fuelled by the mission of building His kingdom for His glory.

It's about Jesus, not a formula

In describing the gospel this way, it is crucial to note that we are not talking about a philosophical system or set of life principles packaged and presented as a certain formula. This is not simply 'six foolproof steps to a happy life'.

Rather, we are talking about the gospel as being the divinely-ordained pathway to a living and loving relationship with Almighty God through the person of Jesus Christ. It is this ongoing relationship with Jesus that brings true life, not merely the adherence to a collection of rules or regulations.

So, the gospel is not just a nice description of God's great ideas but a potent message which opens the way for us to truly know God and be with Him forever. The life-giving power lies not within the story itself but in the God which the story comes to reveal and usher us towards.

The gospel is very much for believers as well

The gospel is both the entry point into the Christian faith and the way through which we continue in it; Christians at any stage of maturity need the outworking of the gospel in their lives as much as they did before they came to initial saving faith.

One leader put it this way: 'The way in is the way on'[6]. In our continuing walk with the Lord, we don't move beyond the gospel but we progress ever deeper into it. We need to be reminded of the gospel each and every day lest we forget the great truths that can sustain and empower us.

This book seeks to repeatedly direct believers themselves to the gospel, and hence to an ongoing vibrant relationship with God, as the very basis on which their daily lives can and should be lived.

What do I mean by 'mental health'?

Mental ill-health

Considering first what is meant by mental ill-health (or 'mental health issues'), it may be useful to think about the following different categories:

1) Mental disorders

This refers to conditions and illnesses which have been carefully studied and categorised[7] and which often, though not always, have a clearer genetic/neurobiological contribution to their development and persistence (e.g. schizophrenia, bipolar affective disorder, major depressive illness, more serious forms of anxiety disorders, eating disorders, severe personality disorders, organic brain diseases, certain kinds of alcohol and/or drug-related problems, autistic spectrum disorder, dementia etc.).

At this level, an appropriate mental health professional can make a clinical diagnosis which should then inform treatment based upon current, scientifically-informed best-practice guidelines. Management of the condition will not uncommonly require input from a multidisciplinary team and involve a range of treatments possibly including psychiatric medication, structured psychological therapy and specific social/occupational interventions focused on improving the person's symptoms as well as their overall level of functioning.

2) 'Problems in living'

This refers to the host of psychological and emotional difficulties that can be commonly experienced as part of living in a world that regularly throws up many challenges and pressures. It includes milder forms of anxiety and depression, uncontrolled anger, genuine hurt, guilt and shame, low self-esteem etc. which can arise from past unresolved conflict (e.g. problems in upbringing, adverse events, major disappointments etc.), current situational stressors (e.g. in the areas of work, family life, finances etc.) and problems in interpersonal relationships.

The level of distress and functional impairment that is experienced may or may not be to the extent that professional help from within the mental health system is indicated and there is a possibility that counselling (outside of statutory mental health services), self-help resources and/or the support provided by family, friends and the church community could aid the person in making significant progress.

3) Spiritual struggles

This refers to the kinds of problems that might arise whenever the focus of struggle pertains to spiritual matters. This could include the angst and confusion of someone who is trying to find a lasting sense of identity, meaning and purpose[8]. There can be particular conflicts emerging during a Christian's walk of faith e.g. anxiety regarding the assurance of salvation, defeating patterns of besetting sin, the discouragement of unknown or unfulfilled ministry calling, unexplained and unrelenting suffering in the midst of faithful service, the hindrances of active spiritual opposition etc.

An individual trying to work through these issues may well first present to a pastoral counsellor/spiritual director or a more mature believer who can understand the specific nature of the difficulties and provide relevant guidance; it would certainly be of additional benefit if the person seeking to help had some wider and more in-depth understanding of mental health problems in general.

The above categories have of course been only broadly distinguished; in reality, there can be much overlap between the presenting problems and in some cases, uncertainty as to the actual underlying 'diagnoses'. Furthermore, people often present with a range of difficulties and it would not be uncommon for someone to be battling with issues pertaining to all three of the areas described at the same time. In other circumstances, different issues may be a focus of challenge at different times, and it would not be improbable that someone will face an area over and over again in a repeated, cyclical manner, hopefully achieving a bit more progress each time the struggle is gone through.

Definition of mental health (incorporating a Christian view)

Mental health is not simply the absence of any mental health difficulty.

The World Health Organisation (WHO) defines mental health as:

> *'A state of wellbeing in which every individual realizes his or her own potential, can cope with the normal stresses of life, can work productively and fruitfully, and is able to make a contribution to her or his community.'*[9]

This is very helpful, and makes the point that mental health embraces a wider view which involves an overall sense of health and includes social and functional components.

I find it helpful to think of mental health as involving wellbeing and growth in the following overlapping areas, with an extension of the above definition to include Christian aspects:

1) Thoughts, feelings and behaviours

Good mental health involves having patterns of thought (including attitudes and beliefs) which are, as far as possible, balanced and realistic, not fraught with apprehension and worry or overly negative and pessimistic.

Feelings (emotions) that arise are appropriate to specific situations and generally stable over time; they can be honestly experienced without undue awkwardness and freely expressed as part of open communication.

Behaviours, which are directly influenced by a person's thoughts and feelings, are positive and purposeful, not repeatedly self-defeating or destructive. On the whole, there is an absence of excessive, distressing, function-impairing levels of stress, anxiety, fear, depression, guilt, shame etc.

2) Relationships

There is a good relationship with oneself in terms of adequate self-awareness, a healthy self-concept and a clear sense of who one is as a unique, authentic individual. There is an ability to relate well in a variety of social situations and across the spectrum of interpersonal intimacy. Longer-term close relationships are characterised by mutual respect, ever deepening communication and sacrificial self-giving. From a Christian perspective, there is a real and vibrant relationship with God that is being worked out and made evident through the practicalities of everyday life.

3) Level of day-to-day functioning

The person is capable of functioning on a day-to-day basis in terms of basic activities of daily living such as self-care, time management, and maintaining suitable accommodation and financial stability. They are able to put in place and sustain structured, purposeful activity e.g. education and/or work as well as interest and leisure pursuits which combine together to bring a sense of identity, meaning and purpose to life. As they progress in life, there is the possibility of discovering deeper fulfilment in terms of realising their specific calling and vocation, based upon their giftings and abilities; they are able to, at least in some degree, experience what psychologists have called 'flow'[10].

4) Resilience (including conflict resolution)

This involves the capacity to live with imperfection, mystery and other unresolved issues at the time. There is an intentional approach to the ongoing internal struggles that they may be facing; weaknesses are acknowledged and are being worked on gradually without undue guilt or shame and with a willingness to seek outside help if necessary. The external challenges of life are handled directly rather than being fearfully avoided. Interpersonal conflict is approached in a way that leads to appropriate resolution. There is a hopeful perseverance in the face of the inevitable trials and sufferings of life, undergirded by a faithful gratitude for what can be perceived as blessings in the midst of difficulty.

5) Character and maturity

This may be construed as being fundamental to a Christian definition of mental health. All the other aspects of mental wellbeing feed into this, and are influenced by it. The goal of the Christian life is to become more and more conformed to the character of Christ Himself, to develop a level of holistic integrity that has been shaped by the empowering work of the Holy Spirit.

Holiness becomes much more important than happiness. Indeed, the more a person grows in godly character and maturity, the greater will be the ability to experience the kind of deep peace and joy that arises from a clear conscience and goes beyond transient pleasure dependent on external circumstances.

The late Dallas Willard, a respected Christian philosopher and teacher, has richly blessed the community of believers with his writings on the deeper dynamics of the spiritual life. In relation to life direction and priorities, one of his helpful nuggets of wisdom is:

> *The most important thing in your life is not what you do; it's who you become. That's what you will take into eternity.*[11]

The definition of mental health presented here is by no means perfect or exhaustive although I believe it will be useful as we discuss throughout the book the potential positive impact of the gospel on these five areas.

Important caveats

It is vital to note that we are definitely not talking about mental health as being a state of problem-free perfection. And I certainly do not want to create the impression that a mentally healthy person is characterised as someone who is always happy and cheerful – that could indeed be quite annoying to those who have to live with such a person.

I appreciate that God does exhort and enable believers to be joyful in all situations (see Rom. 12:12; Phil. 4:4; 1 Thess. 5:16 etc.) but this profound sense of all things being well in one's soul because of the recognition of God's overarching sovereignty is not the same as having nice and positive feelings all the time.

Some, indeed a significant proportion of, mental health conditions (particularly the more biologically-driven mental disorders) are going to be lifelong conditions for which the expectation of 'cure' is not realistic and which hence need to be managed as best as possible, like a lot of physical illnesses such as asthma, diabetes, chronic heart disease, kidney failure, arthritis etc.

In these cases, optimum mental health may mean achieving the best symptom control possible along with as much quality of life as can be attained, acknowledging that the mental illness in no way precludes a fulfilling and productive life. In these situations, it is hoped that the truths of the gospel well-applied can help sufferers endure difficulty with much grace, enhance their capacity to embrace all of life's possibilities, and be a blessing to others who struggle to hold on to hope for a better future.

There is the art of 'being well whilst being ill'; the testimonies of those living with chronic and even debilitating conditions, of how they have found a more profound reality of God in their suffering, are among the most powerful and inspiring[12]. Great is the God-glorifying contentment of those who have learnt how to be the most honest and best they can be, in whatever circumstances they find themselves in, by the grace of God.

The apostle Paul writes in Phil. 4:11-13:

> *Not that I speak in regard to need, for I have learned in whatever state I am, to be content: I know how to be abased, and I know how to abound. Everywhere and in all things I have learned both to be full and to be hungry, both to abound and to suffer need. I can do all things through Christ who strengthens me.*

Relating the gospel to mental health

Making the application

The central message of this book is that the gospel is relevant to all areas of a person's life, including the mental, psychological and emotional realms, and that a proper understanding and embracing of the gospel can potentially have a positive impact on the health of our minds. This is of course not to say that this is the only or even the most important outworking of the gospel – the gospel is firstly about the glory of God, not our self-fulfilment or even our wellbeing. Nevertheless, it can be exciting and radically transformative to realise how the gospel can relate so aptly to our mental health.

A few general points to note in relation to making this application:

1) It is important to stress that I am not here presenting the gospel as an alternative sufficient treatment for recognised and diagnosable mental disorders which have been extensively researched and for which theoretically-driven, scientifically-established therapies have been developed, and where the management of the condition needs to occur within adequately resourced, well-coordinated mental health services.

This is not to say that the gospel has no relevance to people in this position, but that the proper application of the gospel to mental health needs to occur alongside any necessary psychiatric/psychological interventions that are indicated and provide complementary support to these.

2) The principles in this book will likely be more relevant to the categories of everyday 'problems in living' and the various spiritual struggles that can arise in those seeking after truth as well as those who are already believing; it will be particularly helpful if the reader is already at a place where they earnestly desire to grow in their faith and learn how it can be effectively applied to the very challenges that they are currently facing.

3) I would be very keen that the truths of the gospel as applied to the area of mental health can become embedded in the hearts and

minds of every follower of Christ as part of a general discipleship process. In this way, it is hoped that a good understanding of the richness of the gospel can lead to the establishment of a 'baseline' healthy mindset in the life of a believer prior to the development of psychological/emotional difficulties or crises.

This would thus be taking a more preventative approach which can hopefully render a Christian better ready to cope with and get through personal challenges as and when they arise. The vision is that this would also mean that successive generations of believers can learn and experience the life-changing power of the gospel as the truths are handed down through families and church communities.

And this is of course not the only book to try and describe the life-changing power of the gospel as it relates to psychological and emotional wellbeing; a list of further resources is included in the back.

Summary of the book

To try and get the main message of the book across, the next five chapters (chapters 2-6) have a similar layout.

Each chapter takes a main component of the gospel and breaks it down into further aspects. After each truth is described in more detail, an application to the area of mental health is given i.e. how that particular gospel truth can positively benefit a person's psychological and emotional functioning. I have deliberately tried to make the explanations clear, logical and simple.

Chapter 7 goes on to discuss the necessary appropriate responses to the gospel message which bridge the gap between it being a theoretical theological generality to it becoming a personally experienced reality.

Chapter 8 begins with a summary of the truths and applications of the gospel that were presented in Chapters 2-7. An attempt is made to show how these can collectively have a positive impact on the five areas of mental health outlined above: thoughts, feelings and behaviours; relationships; level of day-to-day functioning; resilience (including conflict resolution); character and maturity. It continues with a key 'take home' message and ends with some final words.

The appendices cover three further relevant topics: who this book is for (including a note to seekers and non-believers), how this book could be used (in terms of individual believers, helpers and churches) and the interface with mental health services (where a collaborative, complementary model of working is advocated).

A prayer

It is my hope that these writings will bring an anointed word to your heart and mind as you read and consider for yourself the wonder of God's grace made known to us through His glorious gospel.

"Father, teach us Your ways
Show us Your Son
Fill us with Your Spirit
Be glorified in all that we are and do

May those who are led to read this
Find truth on which to base their lives
The power to change
And real hope for the future."

Chapter 2

IT'S ALL ABOUT HIM

The gospel is primarily about God.

It starts with His eternal existence and is about His predetermined plans and purposes for all creation, the restoration of a broken world and fallen humanity, leading up to the consummation of His everlasting glory.

This is in stark contrast to the position that man historically had to create God for His own survival needs or as a way of plugging the gaps and explaining the thus far unexplainable, as evolutionary naturalists would advocate.

The gospel is not mainly about us, our needs, our desires. No doubt we receive great benefit and blessing whenever through Jesus Christ we can enter into a life-giving relationship with the God of the universe, but our happiness and satisfaction is not the focus of the gospel: His supreme glory is.

The joyful paradox for us is that great inner freedom can arise whenever we recognise this – that God is God and we are not – and live it out in day-to-day experience.

Consider the following truths of the gospel and their potential applications to the area of mental health:

TRUTH:

God reveals Himself through His Word

There is a God

Eminent scientist and prominent atheist, Richard Dawkins, alongside the British Humanist Association, not long ago caused a stir in the UK by being involved in the sponsorship of advertising signs on London buses that read: 'There probably is no God. Now stop worrying and enjoy your life.' Some supporters of this felt that the word 'probably' was too much of a concession and made a case that 'certainly' (or at least 'almost certainly') should be used instead.

The Bible is unequivocal in its assertion that not only is there a God but that He is very real and present and is at the centre of all that is in existence. Not being a scientific treatise, it makes no attempt to rationally explain the hows and whys of His origin but boldly states that He is ultimate reality from whom everything else in the universe emanates.

There is of course a significant degree of presupposition here, and the assertions of the Bible should no doubt be scrutinised in the light of whether it can be trusted as a reliable and accurate source of truth.

Empirical scientific evidence for the existence of God is unlikely to be forthcoming although the 'evidence' for God needs to also be acknowledged from many other streams of knowledge, not least the historicity of Christ and His resurrection as well as the testimony of seemingly impossible life transformation under the power and influence of a higher being.

He has revealed Himself as great, good, holy

The Word of God provides a revelation of who He is, enough for us to know Him, trust Him and walk in His ways. Several aspects of His character are particularly relevant to the discussion of the gospel contained in this book. Without understanding these, we will struggle to fathom the essential tension that exists between a righteous God and a rebellious creation and His plan to reconcile all things to Himself whilst remaining true to His just nature.

At the outset, we are told that God is the creator and sustainer of the universe, by whom, through whom and for whom all things exist (Gen. 1:1; Neh. 9:6; Jn. 1:1-3; Col. 1:16-17; Heb. 1:2-3). This implies tremendous power and sovereignty. His characteristics are commonly described as:

- God is omnipotent (all-powerful)
- God is omnipresent (all-present)
- God is omniscient (all-knowing)

We are shown that God is good (Ex. 34:6-7; Ps. 34:8; Matt. 7:11; 19:16-17; Js. 1:7) and loving (Jn. 3:16; Rom. 5:8; Gal. 2:20; 1 Jn. 4:8-10). God's goodness has been defined as: 'The final standard of good and that all God is and does is worthy of approval'[1]. Love can be thought of as self-giving relationship directed towards the benefit of others, a combination of attitudes and actions that reflect the very nature of God Himself (Jn. 15:12-13; 1 Cor. 13:4-8; 1 Pet. 4:8).

It is revealed to us that God is holy (Lev. 19:2; Is. 6:3; Heb. 12:14; 1 Pet. 1:16; Rev. 15:4) and just (Deut. 32:4; Ps. 7:11; Is. 45:21; Rom. 9:14; 2 Thess. 1:4-10). This means that He is not simply a benevolent but ineffectual being who just wants to be nice and kind to everyone all the time but that He has righteous standards for His created beings and, in faithfulness to His character, will judge against evil in the world.

He has created us to know Him and made a way for us to do so

There is within the heart of each individual seeker a 'God-shaped vacuum'[2], placed there by his/her maker, which leads to a yearning to be filled with truth and love, the very nature of God Himself. God has revealed Himself to us through His Word as a God who desires to know and relate to His created beings in a personal way. He draws us to Himself even before we have any interest in or inclination towards Him, and makes the way for us to come to Him in spite of our brokenness and imperfection.

There have been interesting developments in the field of neuroscience (specifically the small but growing area of 'neurotheology') where researchers have observed human biological features that may indicate an inherent hardwiring towards the search for a higher being and meaning beyond themselves.

Research is in its early stages and a key question of debate is of course whether this arises intrinsically or whether it is more the result of brain changes caused by social evolutionary processes; nevertheless it is an area to watch out for[3].

The way by which we can come to know God constitutes the essence of the gospel, the divine storyline that runs through the whole Bible and involves the great themes of creation, fall and redemption. In this way of salvation, God achieves the proper restoration and destiny of all things whilst remaining faithful to His mercy and justice.

Through repentance from a sinful, self-directed life and faith in a sacrificial Saviour played out in continual surrender and obedience, we can be made right in God's sight and partake of His empowering grace through the indwelling Holy Spirit. This sets in motion a lifelong transformational process towards Christlike maturity.

APPLICATION:

We can come to know a God who is good

We can know Him personally

God has revealed Himself that He may be known personally in real living relationship, both by individuals and then by those individuals being brought together by His Spirit to form His body of people, the church universal.

To have a personal relationship with God means several things:

- *Communication*: God is not a distant, silent being but a real Person with whom we can communicate i.e. He speaks to us through His Word and Spirit and we connect with Him in our thoughts and prayers.

- *Closeness*: the interaction is real and intimate; He knows the innermost character and desires of our hearts and we can share with him our deepest reflections and yearnings, which we may not be able to reveal to any other human being.

- *Continuity*: the presence of God can be with us on a continuous basis, throughout the course of everyday life and not just on sporadic, special occasions.

An intimate personal relationship with Jesus does not mean an irreverently casual one. Whilst we can come as we are and share the most honest concerns of our heart, we also approach His throne with awe and holy fear, knowing that we are coming to a great and mighty God only through the willing sacrifice of His Son.

The big pieces fall into place

Coming into a personal, relational knowledge of God is coming home to where the very core of our being belongs. Like anything that was fully functioning as intended (e.g. a car providing necessary transport, a domestic appliance aiding efficiency in housework, a mobile gadget facilitating effective communication etc.), in a much greater sense, our lives find their full potential and productivity when we are living in the way that God intends for us.

Existential restlessness can be resolved as we discover identity, meaning, purpose and find our place in this world. We can become known for who we really are, and be cherished by a loving Heavenly Father. The fruit of the Spirit and godly character become a blessed reality and we can give ourselves away in selfless service. There is hope for an eternal future in the presence of the glorious One.

The big pieces of the jigsaw fit into place. Not that we have an answer to every question, but that we can have deeply satisfying responses to the questions of life that really matter; we have the correct lens through which we can view all things in the light of truth. As C. S. Lewis quoted:

> *'I believe in Christianity as I believe that the sun has risen: not only because I see it, but because by it I see everything else.'*[4]

With Christ as the focal point, the picture of this world and our lives makes the most sense. The story is told of the little boy who surprised his father one day (paraphrasing and adapting a sermon illustration by J. John):

> *One Summer afternoon, Ben's father wanted to keep him busy for a while and had the idea of cutting up a map of the world from a magazine to create (a rather complicated) jigsaw. Thinking this would buy some precious moments of relaxation in front of the TV, he left the boy to what he*

thought would take a considerable amount of time. Minutes later, the son bounded into the room declaring rapid completion of the task. Surprised, the father asked how on earth he had completed the puzzle so quickly. The little boy, with a satisfied grin on his face, replied, "When you tore the page out I saw that on the other side was a portrait of a man – I knew that if I could get to put his face together so that I could see it, the rest of the world would fall into place!"

Our faith is in a God who is just

To repeat, it is not that every question is answered; far from it. But every crucial query and longing of the heart can receive a good enough answer as we are supplied with the grace to accept the mystery of things we do not and cannot understand, at least this side of eternity. There is indeed truth in the inward parts and in the hidden part He will make us to know wisdom (Ps. 51:6).

There are a multitude of questions that will understandably perplex and trouble us: what about the futures of those who haven't yet come to believe, and the many who seem disinterested about or antagonistic towards the claims of Christ as being the door to salvation? The death of a child, lifelong disability, cruel accidents, nationwide famine, unjust wars; there is an endless list of apparently senseless suffering which can throw us into despair without a deeper and higher truth that provides an anchor for our souls and light to our path. On the surface, life really does not seem fair at all.

We find comfort and assurance in His enduring character. As believers trying to study and comprehend the nature of God, we can arrive, not necessarily easily, at a point of trusting confidence that God is good and just and that the eternal destinies of all human beings who have walked upon this earth will be determined through the framework of His perfect goodness and justice. We can rest in the knowledge that all things, as unfathomable as some things are (Rom. 11:33), work together for His glory.

TRUTH:

God is the centre of the universe

God is the essence and pinnacle of all existence

It has been said that history is His story. This world makes most sense when we see it within the vista of His eternal perspective. His story of history is unfolding in a way that will in the end bring all things under His subjection (Phil. 2:5-11). It is no accident that our modern calendar is based on the historical fact of Christ's birth (although this is certainly being challenged by some agencies who replace B.C. and A.D. with BCE – 'Before the Common Era' – and CE – 'Common Era' – respectively, thus removing Christ from this central position).

Colossians 1:15-18 declares about the Lord Jesus Christ:

> *He is the image of the invisible God, the firstborn over all creation. For by Him all things were created that are in heaven and that are on earth, visible and invisible, whether thrones or dominions or principalities or powers. All things were created through Him and for Him. And He is before all things, and in Him all things consist. And He is the head of the body, the church, who is the beginning, the firstborn from the dead, that in all things He may have pre-eminence.*

Malcolm Muggeridge (1903-1990), the hugely insightful and influential English ex-soldier, journalist and author, writing in the 1970s, said it so well:

> *We look back upon history, and what do we see? Empires rising and falling, revolutions and counterrevolutions, wealth accumulated and wealth disbursed. Shakespeare has*

*written of the rise and fall of great ones, that ebb and flow
with the moon.*

*I look back upon my own fellow countrymen (Great
Britain), once upon a time dominating a quarter of the
world, most of them convinced, in the words of what is still
a popular song, that 'the God who made them mighty, shall
make them mightier yet.'*

*I've heard a crazed, cracked Austrian (Hitler) announce to
the world the establishment of a Reich that would last a
thousand years. I have seen an Italian clown (Mussolini)
say he was going to stop and restart the calendar with his
own ascension to power. I've heard a murderous Georgian
brigand in the Kremlin (Stalin), acclaimed by the
intellectual elite of the world as being wiser than Solomon,
more humane than Marcus Aurelius, more enlightened than
Ashoka.*

*I have seen America wealthier and, in terms of military
weaponry, more powerful than the rest of the world put
together – so that had the American people so desired, they
could have outdone a Caesar, or an Alexander, in the range
and scale of their conquests.*

*All in one lifetime, all in one lifetime, all gone! Gone with
the wind!*

*England, now part of a tiny island off the coast of Europe,
threatened with dismemberment and even bankruptcy.
Hitler and Mussolini dead, remembered only in infamy.
Stalin a forbidden name in the regime he helped found and
dominate for some three decades. America haunted by fears
of running out of those precious fluids that keeps their
motorways roaring, and the smog settling, with troubled
memories of a disastrous campaign in Vietnam, and the
victories of the Don Quixote's of the media as they charged
the windmills of Watergate.*

All in one lifetime, all in one lifetime, all gone! Gone with the wind!

Behind the debris of these solemn supermen, and self-styled imperial diplomatists, there stands the gigantic figure of One: Because of whom, by whom, in whom, and through whom alone, mankind may still have peace – the person of Jesus Christ.

I present him as the way, the truth, and the life. Do you know Him?[5]

All things exist for His glory; worship is the appropriate response

All things exist for His glory. God did not need to create the universe but did so in order that all creation can behold and reflect the greatness and goodness of God, particularly manifest in the person of Jesus Christ. His creative magnificence can be seen in all that He has made and given life to (Num. 14:21; Ps. 19:1; Dan. 7:14; Matt. 6:13; Lk. 21:27; Jn. 1:14; 17:24; 2 Cor. 3:18). He carries out His plans according to His good pleasure (Eph. 1:5, 9).

Rom. 11:36:

> *For of Him and through Him and to Him are all things, to whom be glory forever. Amen.*

The appropriate response is for us to express our thanksgiving, praise and worship and to stand in awe and wonder at what He has done and is doing (1 Chron. 16:24; Ps. 57:5; Rom. 11:36; Eph. 3:20-21; 1 Tim. 1:17; Heb. 13:20-21; Rev. 4:11).

We were made to worship a perfect Being who is far above ourselves. The book of Psalms gives us plenty of heartfelt words to help us do this. Here is just one section, Ps. 100; join in with this expression of praise!

Make a joyful shout to the Lord, all you lands!
Serve the Lord with gladness;
Come before His presence with singing.
Know that the Lord, He is God;
It is He who has made us, and not we ourselves;
We are His people and the sheep of His pasture.

Enter into His gates with thanksgiving,
And into His courts with praise.
Be thankful to Him, and bless His name.
For the Lord is good;
His mercy is everlasting,
And His truth endures to all generations.

We were created to be utterly dependent on Him

Something happens to us when we are not living as God intended. When we take over the reins of our own lives, it becomes all about us. Our motivations, even without us realizing it, become driven by seeking what we want for ourselves. We live and do things in our own strength which may carry us a certain distance but only get us so far. Frustration, feeling overwhelmed, burnout, depression, even a giving up on life itself etc. are not unsurprising results.

Like a car needing fuel to run and lungs needing air to breathe, we were made to be not independent from God but in dependence of Him; there is a world of difference between the two. We are the creatures and He is the Creator (Rom. 9:20). He is the potter, we are the clay (Is. 64:8). He is the vine, we are the branches; without Him we can do nothing (Jn. 15:5). With Him, we become connected to an everlasting life source that produces fruit for His glory.

John the Baptist summarised the call and mission of the believer so well in Jn. 3:30, which has become a life verse of many a faithful follower of Christ, and which describes the course our lives will take once directed by the Holy Spirit:

"He must increase, but I must decrease."

The Christian walk can be described as a steady journey of self-dethronement, and increasing enthronement of the Lord in the centre of our lives.

APPLICATION:

We can place Him first in our lives

We can come into right alignment with how things were made to be

I believe that we were designed for something bigger than ourselves. I also believe that there is a discontent, a sense of inner incompleteness, even a deep anxiety that can arise when we are at the end of the day living for our own sakes, in our own strength. When that happens, we are seeking and turning to seemingly more attractive sources of satisfaction that offer to provide that which we long for, but which can never truly satisfy.

We were not made to find salvation within ourselves but rather to live:

- For Him – that whatever we do in word or deed, we do it as to the Lord and not to men (Col. 3:17; 1 Cor. 10:31) and
- By Him – that the very desire and ability to live a God-centred life is the result of His grace working in and through us (Gal. 2:20; 5:16-18)

Philippians 3 has become a life passage for me. The great apostle Paul, Pharisee and scholar par excellence, saw everything he had achieved outside of Christ, no small achievements by any standard, as being 'rubbish' (v8). His one desire and goal became

38

'that I may know Him and the power of His resurrection...' (v10a). The pursuit of Christ and His mission became everything to him and so it can and should be with us.

In her compelling and profound book, *When the heart waits*, writer Sue Monk Kidd tells a story gleaned from another source, which I have somewhat modified to illustrate a position that Christians would do well to arrive at:

> *I sat there in awe as the old monk answered our questions. Though I am usually shy, I found myself raising my hand. "Father, could you tell us something about yourself?" He leaned back. "Myself?" he mused. There was a long pause.*
>
> *"My name used to be Me. But now it's You."*[6]

Putting Him first is a real privilege

Surrendering our lives to the King of Kings and Lord of Lords does not have to be done begrudgingly. Although, because of our deeply distorted character and motivations, it will be a struggle to bend our wills to our Maker (a wrestling that carries on throughout our whole lives), it is in actuality a great privilege to be able to do so. It should not lead to a resentful release of personal rights and reputation but rather a delightful submission to the One who is most glorified when we are truly blessed in union with Him.

I grew up in the 1970s when the Star Wars phenomenon first burst onto the scene. I was a fan. I was captivated by the heroes of the light valiantly battling to overcome the dark side of 'the Force'. Whenever travelling at night in the back seat of my parents' car, I would look up at the starry sky and my mind would wonder off to a galaxy far, far away. I would dream of being Luke Skywalker, traversing the universe in a spectacular space jet, successfully defeating evil foes on an intergalactic mission that had cosmic implications.

God invites us to join Him on His mission, an adventure far greater than George Lucas or anyone else in Hollywood could conceive – the salvation of souls and remaking of all creation. A life lived in and for the kingdom of God is a journey of discovery, challenge, growth – more stimulating than anything clever special effects can conjure up! We are enabled to have a sense of being part of something much bigger, working as small parts of the great assembly of His called people. We indeed can have a 'higher calling', to live outside and beyond ourselves, and to do so for all eternity.

At the same time, bringing this right down to a day-to-day level, routine and tedious tasks can become little but significant acts of service and worship when they are done within the context of faithfulness to His leading and guidance in all things. The trials of life, in all their ubiquity and range of severity, can become opportunities for the formation of godly character which will carry value long after we depart from this earth. Everyday life becomes graced by meaning and purpose; true contentment no longer depends on material gain or external achievement.

Putting Him first can bring much relief and joy!

It can be an utter relief to be able to live for God. We no longer need to be or feel in control of things we have no control over. We do not have to search for the strength from somewhere just within ourselves to face and address problems whenever the very resources of heaven are at our disposal, and a graciously omnipotent God is overseeing our care and progress.

I don't know about you, but I have enough on my plate in my tiny little corner of this world. Current personal, family, work, church, social etc. commitments have given me plenty to be getting on with (and unfortunately to really worry about at times as well). But my life is a teeny speck and thank God I am not responsible for the running of other people's lives! I would make a most terrible god, even if all I had to look after was myself!

The amusing tale of Jim Carrey's *Bruce Almighty* gives a humorous and sobering portrayal of the absurdity of man taking the place of God. The last thing we would want to wish for would be to be God!

Years ago, I was casually listening to a radio programme about anxiety in the modern world. The invited expert spoke about her approach to managing the issue in her own life. When feeling under pressure, she would step outside and look upwards at the night sky. The immensity of the universe would remind her of how insignificant and dispensable she was in the grand scheme of things and that God could run the cosmos very well without her, thank you very much. Rather than being a crushing blow to her self-esteem, that realisation freed her to live with an open heart and hands, trusting that God was indeed in charge of all things and knew what He was doing. I find it helpful to think how about dispensable I am in God's sight, yet knowing He still chooses to use and bless me.

Tim Keller writes about the freedom from self-obsession and joy of resting in the opinion and acceptance of God through Christ in an aptly titled booklet, *The freedom of self-forgetfulness*:

> *C. S. Lewis in Mere Christianity makes a brilliant observation about gospel-humility at the very end of his chapter on pride. If we were to meet a truly humble person, Lewis says, we would never come away from meeting them thinking they were humble. They would not be always telling us they were a nobody (because a person who keeps saying they are a nobody is actually a self-obsessed person). The thing we would remember from meeting a truly gospel-humble person is how much they seemed to be totally interested in us. Because the essence of gospel-humility is not thinking more of myself or thinking less of myself, it is thinking of myself less.*
>
> *Gospel-humility is not needing to think about myself. Not needing to connect things with myself. It is an end to thoughts such as, 'I'm in this room with these people, does*

that make me look good? Do I want to be here?' True gospel-humility means I stop connecting every experience, every conversation, with myself. In fact, I stop thinking about myself. The freedom of self-forgetfulness. The blessed rest that only self-forgetfulness brings.[7]

Imagine the freedom and joy of living with:

- No (personal, unreasonable) rights and reputation to uphold, and hence without the pain of being easily offended
- No selfish ambitions, and hence without the suffocating drive to gain success at all costs
- No ultimate resources of my own, and hence without the burden of having it all depend on me, my qualifications, my abilities, my achievements
- No unrealistic expectations, and hence without a gnawing sense that I am always missing something and am never quite good enough
- No need to please others and earn their acceptance at all costs, and hence without the need for pretence and a facade when in the company of other people

Such freedom, such lightness of spirit, such relief of pressure comes when we truly grasp that life is all about Him, not about us, when our deepest needs are met in Christ and we don't have to seek their fulfilment outside of Him, that we are called to receive and give in order to serve and bless others. Only in Christ can we have the security and resource to live like this. It is the best deal ever, an amazing divine exchange; we surrender our wills and in return He gives us of Himself and we partake of His love, joy and peace.

When life is busy and stressful, some of the best days I have (when things seem manageable and I dare say I feel more like an overcomer than a man on a downer) are when it hits me: 'On my own I am and have nothing...in and through Him I have everything; He is indeed all that I have and need and want.' Then it doesn't really matter anymore how my own little life pans out, as long as I am wholeheartedly placing myself in the care of the One who holds my life firmly in His hand and am following Him faithfully.

TRUTH:

God is working out His purposes for all creation

The great big picture

So many challenges arise when we only have partial information available in order to make sense of what is going on and decide upon the best way forward. My wife and I have had the recent experience of trying to help a couple whose marriage is in real difficulty. The wife sometimes talks with mine and the husband sometimes with me but, in spite of repeated invitations, we had not been able to bring both of them to the same room to discuss their problems together and get a clearer picture of what is going on between them. Hence, we were only hearing parts of the story in a disjointed manner, and it was very hard to assist them in finding breakthrough.

Life does not make sense when we fail to have a bigger picture in which to place the snapshot of our own lives. We are unable to see how some events relate to each other, or appreciate how the path of our lives has been directed with certain purpose. We can focus only on the troubles of the present time without a view of hopeful things to come.

God is a master storymaker. He is at work bringing about the restoration of all things to Himself. His redemptive plan encompasses individuals whom He has called together to form a new community (His church) as well as all of creation as a whole[8];

the end result will be an eternal representation of His glory. Everything since the dawn of time is leading up to a stage when His purposes are culminated in a new heavens and earth; redeemed human beings have the privilege of holding a special place in being able to share in the glory that is to come.

His sovereignty and power to work it out

The sovereignty and power of God has been revealed through the person of Jesus Christ. Heb. 1:1-3:

> *God, who at various times and in various ways spoke in time past to the fathers by the prophets, has in these last days spoken to us by His Son, whom He has appointed heir of all things, through whom also He made the worlds; who being the brightness of His glory and the express image of His person, and upholding all things by the word of His power, when He had by Himself purged our sins, sat down at the right hand of the Majesty on high, having become so much better than the angels, as He has by inheritance obtained a more excellent name than they.*

The God who spoke the world into being has the power to bring all things under subjection to His will. He is sovereign over all matters – this can be such a hard, hard thing to believe when we look at the world around us and the apparent meaninglessness of some of its tragic events. And yet the testimony of history and the biblical narrative (including historical prophecies that have been fulfilled and are being fulfilled) provide the sense of a great unfolding story that is building up towards an eventual climax.

The sovereignty and power of God is a crucial doctrine to hold onto, and one which can bring awe and then peace to the soul. R. C. Sproul wrote:

> *"If there is one single molecule in this universe running around loose, totally free of God's sovereignty, then we have*

no guarantee that a single promise of God will ever be fulfilled."⁹

This extends to a personal level; He draws us to Himself

In terms of our individual lives, even when we were dead in our trespasses and sins, He made us alive together with Christ (Eph. 2:1, 5). God initiates, sustains and will bring to completion a marvellous plan of redemption, rescuing sinners by His grace and placing them on a trajectory of increasing understanding and fulfilment involving everlasting divine communion and transformation of character into the image of His Son (Rom. 8:28-30; Eph. 1:3-6; Phil. 1:6; 2 Tim. 1:8-10; 1 Pet. 1:2; 2:9).

God is both a transcendent and majestic being, and someone with whom we can have an intimate and personal relationship, who is interested in the very details of our lives. He looks after the sparrows in the sky and the lilies of the field and knows the number of hairs on our heads (Matt. 6:26, 28-29; 10:29-31).

Some people think it is somewhat presumptuous and rather silly to pray for a parking space or the kind of weather we are hoping for (and certainly for any particular result of a sporting contest!). And whilst this may indeed be trivial in the grander scheme of things, it does reveal a simple trust that God cares about everyday matters however insignificant they appear to be, because in the end they all fit together to work out His will on this earth.

APPLICATION:

We can be assured of His working in our lives

From selfish stuckness to Spirit-led sanctification

Before coming to faith in Christ, due to a combination of several factors (basic temperament, family history, life circumstances etc.), I found that I was always trying to improve myself, presumably because I often didn't think I was good enough the way I was. I aspired after a more pure and spiritual life and remember becoming enamoured with the life and teaching of the Indian leader, Mahatma Gandhi (Richard Attenborough's masterful biopic is still one of my favourite films). It was a story of one self-help effort after another, a frustrating series of, as one preacher puts it, 'self-salvation projects'. I bought lots of books about how to become better at this and the other – but didn't always finish reading them. I did not ever change in the nature and degree that I wanted to.

I was not looking for God (or at least I certainly wasn't aware that what I was actually seeking was God Himself) when He found me in my late teenage years. He drew me to Himself before I had any conscious desire or intention to pursue Him. It did take quite a marked personal crisis to mercifully bring me to the end of myself and introduce me to a radically different way of becoming better (which ironically involved first feeling worse about me on my own). With His help, and much less self-fuelled effort, I began to grow by His Spirit and leave behind unhealthy and immature ways of thinking and behaving.

It is sovereign grace that not only does He call and enable us to have faith, He sustains and completes it as well. He is indeed the author and finisher of our faith (Heb. 12:2), and is far more interested and invested in our growth than we are. He who has begun a good work in us will complete it until the day of Jesus Christ (Phil. 1:6).

Looking back over the years of walking with the Lord, I have regularly believed that one of the greatest gifts that He can give us is a desperate sense of need for Him, a strong desire to know Him, an ongoing, unquenchable hunger and thirst for His truth. With these, our hearts will constantly be turned towards Him in a kind of natural default position that would not be possible prior to the regeneration of spiritual new birth. This is not something we can manufacture ourselves, it is a work of supernatural grace.

No more excessive striving (even as Christians)

It is very possible even for committed Christians who are actively seeking to grow in their faith to become overly preoccupied with how they themselves are doing in their walk with the Lord. Spiritual activities (worship, prayer, Bible study etc.) designed to develop devotional depth and freedom can become an end in themselves and an unhelpful measure of how acceptable they believe they are in God's sight. Our journey of spiritual growth is best undertaken when it is empowered by God Himself and leads to His increasing presence and glory in our lives. Otherwise, the perceived extent of our growth becomes the measure of how approved by God we feel.

One of the common dangers in continuing discipleship is that, once having received grace through faith, we then try to operate by our own good works and transfer self-endeavour back into the daily Christian life i.e. grace in, works ongoing.

Paul the apostle writes about this in the book of Galatians (Gal. 3:2-3):

> *This only I want to learn from you: Did you receive the Spirit by the works of the law, or by the hearing of faith? Are you so foolish? Having begun in the Spirit, are you now being made perfect by the flesh?*

We in fact do not need to strive excessively (by which I mean keep trying harder and harder in our own strength, with increasing feelings of futility) in order to grow and change in the ways that He desires. There is no longer a requirement to be self-focused and self-absorbed about how we are doing in relation to personal growth or the things of God. His Spirit is constantly revealing truth, convicting, challenging, shaping the very thoughts and attitudes of our hearts; He does so at the pace and with the timing that He knows is best for us.

As we trust Him to continue this process, we are enabled to achieve a healthy balance between:

1) Acceptance

On the one hand, as imperfect as we are, we can be content and secure in the knowledge of His approval of us based upon the work of Christ on the cross personally appropriated through repentance and faith; because of what Christ has done, we can be acceptable to Him regardless of what stage of maturity we are at. In Christian terminology, we can walk moment-by-moment in the reality of divine justification (or 'positional sanctification').

2) Change

On the other hand, we are empowered to change and be gradually transformed into the image of Christ. We can at the same time have contented acceptance of who we are at any stage of our journey and have a constant experience of transformative change as guided by the Holy Spirit. In Christian terminology, alongside being freely justified in Christ, we can walk moment-by-moment in the reality of divine transformation (or 'progressive sanctification').

The *Serenity Prayer*, an expression of the heart's desire for truth and power that can support real change, has stood the test of time. I believe this is partly because it encapsulates the necessary tension between acceptance and change, and the need for divine help to suitably negotiate this apparent conflict:

> *'God, grant me the serenity to accept the things I cannot change,*
> *Courage to change the things I can,*
> *And the wisdom to know the difference.'*

Interestingly, some modern psychological research is moving in similar directions e.g. with newer forms of cognitive therapy such as dialectical behaviour therapy and mindfulness-based treatments[10]. There is a realisation that an imperative to change needs to be balanced by a reduction in the pressure to change too quickly, in ways which are not possible or realistic for the person at that moment in time.

An awareness of His timing and guidance in matters of growth towards Christlikeness can also help us guard against what could be called 'spiritual greed'. I think of this as a drive to gain more and more (spiritual) information without allowing sufficient time for personal understanding, application and experience. What may contribute to this is an inability to be content with one's spiritual progress, leading to a kind of anxious insecurity and a felt need to always keep improving oneself.

I reckon I am vulnerable to this. Set me loose in a Christian bookshop and I can return home with volumes of inspirational material which I may never read, let alone apply. Knowing that God is 'in charge of our spiritual growth' (as we take responsibility for it and cooperate with his grace) is liberating – He will guide the process and the content, whatever is necessary to help us gradually conform to the image of His Son; our task and challenge is to trust and obey the leading of His Spirit.

The value of our journeys

I have come to think that the sovereignty of God is a powerful, mind-blowing doctrine. If we really believed it, a radical change in the way we view our lives can follow. For those who love God and are seeking after Him – everything that happens to us is part of a developing divine story which He Himself is crafting. Rom. 8:28 has brought help and hope to many believers:

> *And we know that all things work together for good to those who love God, to those who are the called according to His purpose.*

I find this of particular comfort on days when I am feeling inadequate and ineffective, and when I slip back into that awful habit of comparing myself with others who I think are much more accomplished than myself. As we consider the journey of our lives to date, we can gain an assurance that nothing has been wasted! We are learning and growing in ways which have everlasting value, even though we can't always see that clearly at the time. In spite of what can be very difficult circumstances, we are steadily being transformed on the inside for purposes that are beyond our full comprehension (2 Cor. 4:16-18).

If we adopt the view that God is working out His purposes for mankind, including the purifying and maturing process of individual human hearts, we can face the challenges of life with new and hope-filled perspective. Our problems are not just there to discourage and defeat us; they can be the very things that show up the areas where God wants to work in us, and the very things through which we can persevere in ways that produce life-tested character.

When I am feeling tired and down, perhaps after a particularly taxing period of life, I would sometimes question whether I have made some major mistakes in terms of decisions about work, relationships, church etc. When I am then able to spend time in His presence and allow Him to help correct my perspective, I become appreciative again of how He has led me down certain paths for His higher purposes, even when the way has been rough at times.

A deep rest can come upon us when we realise that He is providing and guiding in very real ways, even in the everyday details of our lives. Our journeys are His journeys in and through us and the paths that our lives take, even if we can't understand why there have been many detours and delays, are the paths that He has destined for us in order that we may do His bidding.

Chapter 3

THE GIFT OF BROKENNESS

Before we can truly appreciate the good news of the gospel, we need to be confronted with the bad news of how things have gone wrong.

The path to knowing God in a very real way often (if not always) begins with a sense of brokenness, a coming to the end of ourselves. Only those who have become aware of their lost state will be open to the Saviour who is seeking for them (Lk. 19:10). Only the sick realise their need for a physician (Matt. 9:12; Mk. 2:17; Lk. 5:31).

I am moved by the story in Lk. 7:36-50 of the sinful woman who finds forgiveness and freedom in the presence of Jesus. She encountered her own dark condition and then came face-to-face with grace personified. Her inward joy of salvation was outwardly expressed in extravagant worship, washing His feet with her tears and anointing them with precious fragrant oil. The Lord captured the essence of the spiritual dynamic at work with His words (v47):

> *"Therefore I say to you, her sins, which are many, are forgiven, for she loved much. But to whom little is forgiven, the same loves little."*

Consider the following truths of the gospel and their potential applications to the area of mental health:

TRUTH:

We live in a broken world

This is not hard to see

It is not hard to see that something is wrong in this world. Evil, injustice, misery and suffering are rampant in all corners of the earth. At a personal level (for those of us insightful enough to recognise it and honest enough to admit it) we are deeply flawed in terms of our thoughts, motivations and actions which naturally steer towards what would best serve our own needs and desires. Truth be told, we have a hard time changing ourselves in the ways we should let alone anyone or anything else around us.

The problem of evil and suffering can be a major stumbling block to reasonable faith for believers, seekers and sceptics alike. To compound the difficulty, it is very hard to justify the terrible deeds that appear to have been done in the name of the Christian religion (the list is well-known and can be rattled off by some, particularly those who are antagonistic to faith: crusades, inquisitions, witch-hunts, bigotry, hypocrisy etc.).

When what we observe around us seems so senseless, it can be easier to adopt a position of agnosticism or atheism whereby the rationale for tragedies of all sorts lies in an ultimate randomness of life events and the cold fact that 'bad stuff just happens'. Or, the best explanation becomes that there is simply no satisfactory, meaningful explanation that can or should be expected.

The Bible presents a coherent explanation

In the face of the reality of a broken world, the Bible presents an explanation that is worth taking seriously. Not that it provides easy or straightforward answers – indeed, many questions need to be asked and explored – but it helps us to have a more comprehensive and full-orbed view of the way things are.

From an initial perfect creation, Genesis 3 sheds light on how things began to go askew at both a universal and personal level. We learn here about the initial presence of a personified evil (the origin of which is beyond the scope of this book although some clues are given in Is. 14:12-15; Ez. 28:12-17) whose intention it was to destroy mankind and usurp his God-given authority over the earth.

The devil in the guise of a serpent deceived man (and woman) who then chose to disobey God, disregarding submission to Him and becoming their own self-reliant masters. This rebellion resulted in a turning away from the light and a broken relationship with their holy Creator which has since been passed down to successive generations (Rom. 5:12-19; 1 Cor. 15:21-22).

The entrance of sin into the world led to the introduction of decay, disease and death and the proliferation of an anti-God world system of thought bent on persuading people to disavow their Maker and lose any semblance of a rightful fear of God – we are currently living in a time when atheism has taken on a more aggressive stance, calling for the abolishment of religion as we know it, which has been deemed utterly unscientific, superfluous to an understanding of the modern world and even downright harmful to society as a whole.

If we apply this understanding to the area of inner struggles, we can appreciate that problems in living could arise from a variety of sources, often in combination with each other. Hence, one way of thinking about the potential causes of problems is:

1) Spiritual conflict i.e. influence, opposition or 'warfare' with the forces of evil (the devil and his demons) and the anti-Christian, humanistic world system which dominates this age and

permeates all that we do in this world (Rom. 8:38; 2 Cor. 10:3-5; Eph. 6:12; Js. 4:4; 1 Jn. 2:15-16).

2) Sin i.e. that which leads us to go our own way in terms of our desires and decisions; the self-righteousness that causes us to lean on our own efforts to try and gain approval from God and others, effectively negating the sacrifice of Christ on our behalf. It includes the giving in to the uncrucified lusts of the flesh (Gal. 5:19-21; Eph. 4:22; Col. 3:5; Js. 4:1-2; 1 Jn. 2:16).

3) Sickness i.e. the effect of a fallen world on human physiological functioning with the subsequent emergence of disease and illness (through genetic mutation, the ageing process, infectious microorganisms, environmental pollutants, physical trauma etc.).

4) Suffering i.e. the need to endure hardships, trials and tribulations (including active persecution) in spite of every attempt to resolve the underlying issue at hand; the often mysterious presence of gross imperfection and apparent injustice, the purpose of which can lie much deeper than we are able or even prepared to think about (this is discussed further in Chapter 6).

5) Shortcomings i.e. failings and weaknesses that arise from a lack of knowledge and/or experience, aspects of immaturity which we need to learn and grow out of rather than spiritual conflict or sin from which we need to be delivered.

Thankfully, the story doesn't end there

In His mercy, God doesn't leave us lost and crushed in our brokenness. He has been about the business of redemption ever since the angels and man fell from grace (as alluded to in Isaiah 14 and Ezekiel 28, and described in the book of Genesis) and has given us a written revelation of the unfolding story, which is being worked out throughout human history, of all things being made new.

With succinctness, bearing in mind the risk of oversimplification, some have summarised the message of the Bible as:

- Genesis 1-2: how things should have been
- Genesis 3: where things went wrong
- Genesis 4 – Revelation 22: how God is making all things right again

His plan of salvation includes ultimate solutions, both now and eventually, for each of the causative problem areas described above. In this present age, the root of evil and sin has been severed through the death and resurrection of Christ. General truth and knowledge is made available to help develop better treatments for the myriad of sicknesses that can befall human beings; some would argue that the power of God is available to bring healing beyond purely natural means. We can be held and sustained in our suffering when it occurs within the context of a life imbued with hope. In the age to come, we can look forward to God's complete dealing with spiritual conflict, sin, sickness and suffering.

An understanding of the transitional stage that we are in now can help us reconcile a world falling apart with a world being fully restored. On the one hand, the kingdom of God is here, in the hearts of His people (Lk. 17:21), and we see signs of His supernatural reality. On the other hand, the kingdom of God is yet to come (Lk. 22:25-27), and we look forward with longing expectation to the day when He will rule and reign in glory. In the meantime, we live in the tension of 'the already and the not yet'.

APPLICATION:

We can assume appropriate responsibility for our problems

An accurate view of the reasons for our difficulties

When people are in difficulty, they understandably want an explanation of how they got into that position in the first place, in the belief that an understanding of that will significantly assist them to get out of their challenging situation. This is of course entirely appropriate (although waiting for a full and complete explanation/understanding of the cause of their problems before doing anything about them is not to be encouraged either – I am often telling patients to start making the recommended changes in their behaviour as soon as possible and as they do so, increased insight arises along the way).

Adopting a biblical perspective enables us to have a more accurate and helpful understanding of the reasons for our difficulties which can provide a basis for focused improvement. It allows us to take a broad view of aetiological factors, and to appreciate the complexity involved in the genesis of even a 'simple' looking scenario (through an interplay of the potential causes mentioned above). In contrast to secular formulations, a Christian view takes into account the not insignificant influence of non-physical contributors.

At the same time, it would be important to say that sometimes, if not often, the cause and purpose of our struggles are shrouded in mystery and the whole ordeal appears senseless and unnecessary. During periods like that, the Christian believer is drawn to the presence of God to seek and find sustaining grace when the reasons for painful things are not at all clear.

Appropriate responsibility-taking

When we are hurting and in need of real relief, it is natural to look for someone or something to blame for the predicament that we find ourselves in; we do this both consciously and unconsciously. In this matter, we need to ensure that we have 'balanced responsibility' which allows us to experience healthy guilt (which involves a conviction of the Holy Spirit) and protects against unhealthy/neurotic guilt (which can be associated with crippling shame[1]).

There are two traps that we can fall into when thinking about why we struggle with problems in living and where the burden of responsibility lies:

1) Taking too little responsibility

Here we fail to realise how our own self-centred bias leads us to make unwise and harmful choices which result in problematic consequences. There is an inability to take the necessary personal responsibility for one's own actions, and a choosing instead to inappropriately blame other people and external factors for present difficulties.

- *An outwardly successful businesswoman battling with addiction to alcohol refuses to accept that she has a problem and needs to take responsibility for seeking help.*

- *A frustrated father has repeated clashes with a seemingly rebellious son without giving any consideration to how he may be regularly provoking his child to anger.*

- *An overworked minister grows increasingly impatient and angry with his 'demanding' congregation whilst remaining unaware of his tendency to take on too many unnecessary tasks for fear of displeasing others and needing their approval.*

2) Taking too much responsibility

Here we assume that most if not all of our difficulties are in some way related to internal deficiencies within ourselves. There is an inability to recognise that the causation of problems is often complex and multifactorial, and that their own role in the matter may be of much less significance than they initially thought.

- *A depressed teenager who suffered abuse as a child believes that it was primarily because of some inherent fault in himself that led to it happening as opposed to the obvious wickedness of the perpetrator.*

- *An anxious mother struggling to cope with an apparently underachieving child feels that it is all her fault that the child hasn't 'turned out right'.*

- *A discouraged pastor whose congregation doesn't appear to be growing concludes that it is solely his inadequacy in ministry that is the reason for that.*

The appropriate balance of responsibility can be very hard for a person to figure out on their own. This is when they would need the input of an informed, skilled, compassionate helper to bring a truer perspective to their struggle, and clearer focus as to what areas need to be addressed and how best to approach them.

There is true hope when the real issues can be tackled

We instinctively know that problems persist when their roots remain. Unlike others, I have no love for gardening and try and do as little of it as possible (which is why we have only a small patch of greenery in our otherwise cemented garden). But even I know that the weeds which regularly sprout in our back yard need to be properly dug out from deeper down or else they will just keep appearing.

It must be devastating to be given a medical diagnosis of a physical condition which is progressively deteriorating but for which there is no curative treatment. Similarly, to struggle with internal conflict and distress with little concept of the key reasons for the dilemma or, worse still, with no hope of resolution, would be soul-destroying.

The good news is that the Word of God, illuminated by the Spirit

of God, helps us to make sense of our difficulties and how we can face each of them. In some areas of struggle, there
are things we can think about and believe and do differently which will have a positive impact. In others, ready solutions may not be forthcoming and in those cases we can equally turn to God for the grace to endure.

TRUTH:

Our sin is a major problem

A focus on one key area

I want to focus for a moment on the issue of sin in relation to it being a significant contributory element of personal life struggles. This not to suggest that it is always the most important consideration in a particular situation although the effects of sin are pervasive and I believe can be viewed as being relevant in some way to all human issues.

Sin can be defined as missing the mark, failing to measure up to the standards for thought and behaviour set by God Himself and revealed throughout His holy Word. It is the ingrained defiant attitude that does not wish to submit to the desires and will of our Creator, even though His intentions toward us are pure and good; it is about going our own way and being the lord of our own lives.

It is reflected in an inherent tendency towards self-focus and fruitless introspection (someone helpfully pointed out that what lies in the middle of 'sin' is the letter/word 'I'). It is believing that we can be good enough for God (and others) by what we can achieve in our own strength and by our own efforts. It includes the more overtly sinful actions and manifestations of a sinful heart (Gal. 5:19-21; Eph. 4:19, 31; Col. 3:5-9).

A sinful nature is unfortunately our default position by virtue of being a descendent of Adam. We are born and develop with a natural pull towards self-centredness (ask any parent to confirm this from first-hand experience of raising children!) that if not broken and redeemed will lead to a life in persistent ignorance of or rebellion against God[2].

We can consider several aspects of sin as it is experienced by all people in everyday life, all of which may in some way have a part to play in the development of personal and interpersonal difficulties:

1) <u>Sinful desires</u> i.e. the inclinations of our hearts to depend on our own strength, consider ourselves first, disregard the needs of others, lust after that which is not rightfully ours etc.

2) <u>Sinful reactions</u> when those desires are not fulfilled i.e. our anxiety, anger, scheming, manipulation etc. whenever what we long for does not come to pass and appears to be beyond our ability to obtain.

3) <u>Sinful actions by us</u> (against others) i.e. the times when we cross the line and act out sinful desires and motives, fulfil our need for illicit pleasure, and deliberately (or sometimes unknowingly) hurt others and cause injustice.

4) <u>Sinful actions by others</u> (against us) i.e. the times when we are at the receiving end of the sinful attitudes and behaviours or others causing ourselves to feel hurt, discouraged, betrayed etc.

5) <u>Sinful reactions to sin by others</u> against us i.e. when we react in ways which are themselves sinful e.g. anger growing into bitterness and resentment held onto far longer than is necessary or healthy; there is a real danger that this 'tit-for-tat' pattern can spiral into a prolonged vicious cycle of negative emotion, to the detriment of all parties involved.

6) <u>Sinful (the secular terminology would be 'maladaptive') coping mechanisms</u> to initial problematic experiences/behaviours e.g.

turning to the misuse of alcohol or drugs to manage the distress caused by unresolved anxiety or grief, medicating ourselves with lustful pleasure to cover up problems with intimacy and loneliness, outbursts of anger towards others when frustration feels intolerable etc.

The potential impact of sin on mental health

How does sin contribute towards actual problems in living? In one sense, the basic sinful stances of pride and unbelief can lead to a whole host of other sins. Sin can have its impact via direct consequences (e.g. abuse leading to damaged emotions and personality) or secondary issues (e.g. guilt arising out of transgression of God's will; Ps. 32, 38, 51 etc.).

(In the latter regard, appropriate guilt arising from true conviction of sin can be a stimulus to necessary change in thinking, attitudes and behaviour as opposed to excessive guilt based upon false assumptions of responsibility.)

Jay Adams presents a useful model of how sin can taint a human being at different levels[3]:

1) Presentation problems: the presenting psychological/ emotional states; the subjective experience which the person feels is the main troublesome issue (often presented as a cause when really an effect).

2) Performance problems: the impact of the person's struggle on their behaviour and (interpersonal) functioning (often presented as an effect when really a cause).

3) Preconditioning problems: the habitual thought and behaviour patterns which form the underlying disposition of the person and which influence the way in which they deal with external circumstances and life crises.

This sets us up for salvation through a Saviour

As we have been saying, God does not leave us without hope. He has made a way for sin and all its manifestations to be dealt with; He has sent us His Son to be our Saviour through His death on the cross and resurrection to life.

Col. 2:13-14:

> And you, being dead in your trespasses and the uncircumcision of your flesh, He has made alive together with Him, having forgiven you all trespasses, having wiped out the handwriting of requirements that was against us, which was contrary to us. And He has taken it out of the way, having nailed it to the cross.

We will look more closely at what Jesus has done for us, including how He has dealt with the problem of sin, in the next chapter.

APPLICATION:

A sin paradigm enables a Saviour solution

The helpfulness of thinking about sin

It would not be surprising to think that a focus on sin is antithetical to the building up of healthy self-esteem and hence has a negative impact on a person's mental health. In the minds of some, sin is a taboo subject that has no place in the thinking about people and their problems.

Indeed, if this whole topic is not handled well and not presented in the appropriate spirit of truth and love, the listener can quite understandably feel judged and condemned and possibly even

62

more hopeless about the prospect of freedom from besetting problems.

However, properly understood and applied, adopting a sin paradigm can potentially be the most truthful, loving and helpful way to approach certain problematic situations as this can pave the way for breakthrough into a depth of liberty previously unattainable or even thought possible. A realisation of our sin and its effects leads us to come in repentance and faith to the Saviour who has made a way for it to be effectively dealt with. So, an appropriate focus on sin is not harshly condemning but powerfully freeing.

Imagine someone saying to you: "I know what an essential part of your problem is – you have an inherent tendency to go your own way, disregard proven wisdom, engage in self-destructive behaviour and often do all this without realising that it is happening (or worse, thinking you are actually doing quite ok). Unfortunately, you are like this from the day you were born, your parents were like it, it is permanently hardwired into your system and you are just going to have to learn to cope with it and stay out of trouble as best you can. There is really nothing that can be done about the core of this issue." Praise God that that is not the situation we find ourselves in in Christ.

How does our Saviour help us in our sin? We revisit these theological realities:

1) Justification: divine justice is upheld through the punishment for sin being borne by another on our behalf, making the way for us to be acceptable in the eyes of a holy God as we become graciously clothed in the righteousness of Christ (more about this in Chapter 4).

2) Sanctification: as we surrender to Him, the Holy Spirit gets to work changing our thoughts, affections, desires, behaviours etc., helping us to become less vulnerable to the pull of temptation and more fixated on the pursuit of holiness (more about this in Chapter 5).

3) <u>Glorification</u>: we can eagerly look forward to a time when sin will fade away in the blaze of His consummated glory (more about this in Chapter 6).

The need and ability for genuine repentance

Repentance is the deliberate turning away from sin and determined resolution, by the grace of God, to live according to His ways. It comprises heart attitude and outward action. It involves healthy grief over sin, honest confession, and the asking of forgiveness from God (and others).

This is the appropriate response to the seriousness of sin and the way in which He can lead us experientially into personal freedom. If we are to be truly righteous in His sight, sin cannot be ignored, downplayed or dabbled with. 1 Jn. 1:9 lays out His path of forgiveness and cleansing:

> If we confess our sins, He is faithful and just to forgive us our sins and to cleanse us from all unrighteousness.

God Himself enables us to genuinely repent. The Holy Spirit brings precious conviction without which we will remain oblivious to the reality and implications of our sin (Jn. 16:8). It is the very goodness of God that leads us to repentance (Rom. 2:4). He allows us to experience godly sorrow that produces repentance, leading to life-giving salvation (2 Cor. 7:9-10).

The danger of excluding a sin paradigm

My contention here is that incorporating a biblical view of sin into our conceptualisation of personal problems is not just positively helpful but is essential.

Without this, we can falter in terms of taking right responsibility for our thoughts, feelings and behaviour and miss the opportunity to receive grace for some of our deepest struggles. We can get into the habit of blaming everything else for our difficulties without effectively addressing the real heart issues.

Perhaps what can be even more sinister for a Christian is that without a sin and Saviour paradigm, we are bound to try and save ourselves: to gain acceptance from God through something that we have to generate from within ourselves, to try and modify negative patterns of thinking and acting without wisdom and strength from above, to anxiously hope that at the end of the day the scale of our life accomplishments will tip ever so slightly in the right direction.

This creates a pressure to achieve, perform, strive in order to feel good enough; the angst of not knowing for sure if our efforts have been enough, the depression of mood that comes from realising how far short we fall in relation to the standards God has set and the shame that prevents us from being honest about our failures can all become our constant companions.

Personal recovery and growth becomes all about us, trying to get better ourselves, eventually burning ourselves out; anyone who has seriously tried to change themselves along godly lines will know the frustration I am talking about here. Faced with a mountain of hard challenges, it is scary, not to mention impossible, being all on our own.

TRUTH:

God allows us to have a sense of our own brokenness

A vision of His ways

Is. 55: 8-9:

"For My thoughts are not your thoughts,
Nor are your ways My ways," says the Lord.
"For as the heavens are higher than the earth,
So are My ways higher than your ways,
And My thoughts than your thoughts."

Rom. 11:33:

Oh, the depth of the riches both of the wisdom and
knowledge of God! How unsearchable are His judgements
and His ways past finding out!

Col. 1:27:

To them God willed to make known what are the riches of
the glory of this mystery among the Gentiles: which is
Christ in you, the hope of glory.

The way God sees and does things is often so alien to the human mind. I am constantly being surprised by how He works, in ways which turn out to be so much more wise and fruitful than I, or anyone else, could come up with. I have learnt long ago that the depth of the riches of His wisdom and knowledge is immensely vast, and that life is an ongoing journey of discovery of who He is and how He operates in this world.

I have come to realise that, if all things exist for His glory, the way He is going to be most glorified in and through us is when we are thoroughly filled with His presence and life such that the very character of Christ becomes formed in us. And it is through brokenness that this fullness of the Spirit can be received and maintained. I believe that when we are truly glorifying Him, we have the benefit of real joy and fulfilment ourselves, and that in turn brings Him further glory.

Reformed pastor/theologian, John Piper, has (now quite famously) quoted:

'God is most glorified in us when we are most satisfied in Him.'

To this I would humbly add:

'We are most satisfied in life when He is being most glorified in and through us.'

Defining brokenness

Brokenness is the humble realisation that without Him we are and can do nothing (Jn. 15:5). It is an experiential acknowledgement that in Him we can do all things (Phil. 4:13). It is acknowledging the depth and seriousness of sin; when outwardly successful and capable people realise that they are the chief of sinners (1 Tim. 1:15). It is humility before an awesome God, the precursor to being lifted up by Him (Js. 4:10). It is when a person is ready to be used for His glory, seeking no honour for him or herself (2 Tim. 2:21).

The experience of brokenness can hurt deeply but the rewards of true brokenness are huge, as A. W. Tozer remarked:

'Whom God will use greatly, He will wound deeply.'

I am not suggesting here that God deliberately seeks to wound us, but that He does allow certain things to come into our lives and happen to us, which He will in the end use for His purposes and glory.

Brokenness can come through many paths and affect any area of our lives (often in combination):

- Physical: illness, disability, death/bereavement etc.
- Psychological: mental disorders, low self-esteem, other problems in living etc.
- Social: broken relationships, loss of a job, financial problems etc.

- Spiritual: besetting sin, a 'thorn in the flesh', spiritual oppression etc.

He brings us to the end of ourselves for His glory and our benefit

Thus, He is actively overseeing the course and events of our lives such that we have the opportunities to come to the end ourselves and have our pride and self-reliance broken, in order that the fullness of God Himself may reside in us and be manifest through us, all for His glory.

It is not that God is the author of evil or meaningless suffering but that in His wisdom and sovereignty He ordains and allows the circumstances of our lives to shape us in ways that allow Him to be most glorified in and through us, and for us therefore to be most satisfied in Him.

For the seeker of Christ, difficult things are not poor fate, bad karma, vengeful retribution etc. but His plan to make us more like Him (and less of ourselves). When we feel empty, lost, weak, hopeless etc. is the very time that we may be most open and receptive to God and His good grace.

God can use every possible life situation (especially the difficult ones) to create a greater sense of brokenness within us and hence more space for His presence and grace to come in and fill. With renewed vision, the trials of life can be seen as gifts from above that make it possible for us to become less of ourselves and more of Him. One of the most reassuring verses in the Bible for believers, Rom. 8:28, was written in the context of suffering.

The way God works with us is not cruelty but true love from a Heavenly Father who wants the best for us (Heb. 12:5-7). It can be painful at the time but the rewards in terms of character, maturity and fruitfulness are vast and far-reaching; there is no greater gift than to receive God Himself.

As a child, I can remember my mother repeatedly reminding me about the importance of humility in this life. Without Christ, I think this may have developed into a false sort of pride where I was excessively denigrating myself without knowing that I needed to receive grace in place of my weakness. Little did I know though, that God was using even this early nurturing to set the scene for an appreciation of the value of divinely-inspired brokenness.

Note: the breaking of the self by the working of God's Spirit is of course not to be confused with issues and problems arising from wilful disobedience or an unrenewed heart that is engaging in regular sinful behaviour. In these situations, our prayer should be that God's mercy will be revealed and we will have an appropriate conviction that leads to godly repentance and a correction of our ways.

APPLICATION:

Brokenness can be a gateway to grace

There can be great blessing in our brokenness and pain

So, the very problems in living that we struggle with could be the very things that bring us closer to God. Through the path of brokenness, we learn lessons we can learn no other way. Our eyes are opened to the weakness of our own selves which becomes a precursor for His strength to flow in and through us. He can come and fill the emptiness and longing that brokenness creates.

With this understanding, we no longer need to fear our difficulties/struggles/trials but see them as instruments of transformation. We can embrace them as the very things that will bring us closer to God and deeper in Him. In fact, the more challenging a situation is, the more grace that we stand to experience and the better the training in righteousness we receive!

Down the line, those very areas of weakness are the very things that He can use for His glory. With due consecration to the Lord, shy, stammering youths have been made into anointed preachers of the Word. Down and out convicts have found grace to plunder hell and minister salvation to others. Those who have known the darkness and despair of mental breakdown have been restored and become effective wounded healers.

How does this work in practice?

I believe that the Holy Spirit, in the midst of ordinary, everyday life as well as during more concentrated periods of trials and testing, actively teaches those who have eyes to see and ears to hear and are willing to learn a number of key lessons:

1) There is a breaking down

He is determined to strip away all that would stand in the place of us loving God with all our heart, soul, strength and mind:

a) *The primary call to know Him*

It becomes ever clearer to us that the most important thing in life is to know Him and walk in His will; everything else is directed towards this goal. We realise that eternal life rests upon knowing the only true God, and Jesus Christ whom He has sent (Jn. 17:3).

b) *He is all we have/need/want*

Blessed is the man who comes to know the sufficiency of Christ, that at the end of the day, He is all we have/need/want. Nothing else will satisfy the longing of our hearts apart from worshipful intimacy with Him. We can resonate with the psalmist that our one desire is to dwell in the house of the Lord all the days of our lives (Ps. 27:4).

c) *We can of ourselves do nothing*

We are allowed to experience how disappointing and dead it feels to be living in our strength, to be trying to achieve His purposes without His power; it is another of His profound blessings to go through the dysphoria associated with feeling inadequate about and overwhelmed with what we have to face without His enabling[4]. We are brought to the liberating truth that only as we abide in Him, and He in us, we bear much fruit; for without Him we can do nothing (Jn. 15:5).

d) *No faith even in our faith*

As we draw nearer to Him, we learn that we are dependent on Him even for our ability to come close; otherwise we can fall into the mistake of trusting in our methods of knowing Him rather than in God Himself. We are continually reminded that even the faith through which we receive His grace comes as a divine gift, not of works, lest anyone should boast (Eph. 2:8).

2) There is a building up

Alongside breaking down in us all that is not of Him, He builds us up by and with His grace in an act of glorious divine exchange:

a) *Strength in weakness*

It is one of the most faith-affirming experiences to see God move in and around us during times when we feel helpless and weak within ourselves. And yet He calls us to a life of regular moments like these, where we work from a position of rest and receiving, that He may be glorified as the One from whom all good things flow. We have the marvellous privilege of knowing His sufficient grace, as His strength is made perfect in our weakness (2 Cor. 12:9).

b) *We can put on the new man*

As we are broken down, we are not left without any hope or bearings. Rather, we have the opportunity for personality transformation beyond our highest imagination due to the sanctifying work of the Holy Spirit. We are enabled to put off the old way of doing things and put on the new man in Christ which was created according to God, in true righteousness and holiness (Eph. 4:20-24).

c) *Seen and unseen impact*

A life that is broken and built up by the Lord is one that He can use to spread the living knowledge of Him everywhere we go. This sometimes escapes superficial observation: the annals of Christian service are rife with stories of prolonged faithful ministry without apparent obvious results at the time, only for the real fruit to be seen after they have passed on. One of my heart's desires is that people will look at me and wonder how on earth an ordinary and unimpressive man can doing anything of worthy significance – and to bypass me and glorify my Father in heaven (Matt. 5:16).

d) *Joy in trials*

One of the hardest, most counter-intuitive lessons that He teaches us about the spiritual life is that of having joy in all circumstances (Phil. 4:4; 1 Thess. 5:16). The more we are stripped down and surrendered to Him, the better able we will be to respond with a joyful attitude when the pressure is on, and if we can learn to do that, there is very little that we won't be ready for (Js. 1:2-4). I discuss this vital concept further in Chapter 6.

A story of redemption

When a sobering revelation of our own sin and need for grace is followed by a clear vision of His redeeming power, the chains fall off and the spirit soars. The gospel has been described as knowing how bad the sin of man is, and how good the grace of God is:

Seeing things as they are

A young lady was deeply troubled in her heart and mind. She felt at a loss as to how to proceed. A servant of the Lord, known for His compassion and insight, was visiting her town and she went to seek counsel from Him. After their first (relatively short) discussion, he left the vicinity, stating that he would be back in a week's time. That week, the woman's family noticed that she seemed even more downcast, frequently tearful, struggling to cope with everyday responsibilities. They were increasingly concerned and tried to bring the matter up with her but she was as yet unable to speak about what was going on in her soul.

The following week, the pastor returned and a further conversation was had. This was again quite brief. He went on his way and said that he wasn't planning to return as a matter of routine but could be contacted if she felt a further meeting would be helpful. For that week, and subsequently, there was a radiance in her face, a lightness in her step, a quiet confidence in the way she went about her work, a new assurance that emerged.

Her family were intrigued. After several weeks had past, they could contain their questions no longer and sat her down to find out what had happened. The lady spoke about the two encounters. She said that at the first meeting, the minister had listened to her dilemma of never feeling good enough, always wanting to please others, not knowing how she could ever be approved by God.

He said little but asked her to earnestly pray a prayer over the coming week: "Lord, show me myself". This had led to convicting insight, and an acknowledgement that she hadn't realised how bad she actually was apart from the grace of God. Her heart was broken.

The following week, the wise counsellor listened again. The woman's heart was broken, but so was a spirit of self-righteousness; gone was the entrenched belief that all she must do was try harder, better, longer, with as much inner strength as she could muster. He then asked her to pray again, this time with a switch in focus: "Lord, show me Yourself".

In the weeks to come, the grace of God became real to her. The despair of brokenness was met by a deliverance into the arms of an all-sufficient Saviour. Endless striving to achieve and perform was replaced by the solid peace of being deemed good enough because of what somebody much better and greater had already done on her behalf. She was free to be as weak as she really was because God Himself could then be her strength.'[5]

It has been said that a true appreciation of the gospel arises whenever we come to realise how bad we can be, and at the same time comprehend how good the redeeming grace of God is. Tim Keller puts it this way:

'The gospel says you are more sinful and flawed than you ever dared believe, but more accepted and loved than you ever dared hope.'

Chapter 4

WHAT JESUS HAS DONE

The work of Jesus Christ on the cross is a central component of the gospel.

It has been said that Jesus is the only religious leader who was born to die. The whole of the Old Testament points towards and builds up to the time of the coming of the Messiah who would take away the sins of the world. The movement of the gospels show the Saviour's steadfast progression towards Jerusalem to fulfil His God-ordained mission of dying on the cross.

And Jesus is the only key religious leader of past times who is still alive today! The resurrection of Christ provides firm historical evidence for the truth of Christianity[1]. It is the basis on which we can know that the willing sacrifice of Jesus on our behalf was accepted and that the life-giving power of Almighty God is absolutely real. As Paul puts it in 1 Cor. 15:14, 17:

> *And if Christ is not risen, then our preaching is empty and your faith is also empty...*
>
> *...And if Christ is not risen, your faith is futile; you are still in your sins!*

Consider the following truths of the gospel and their potential applications to the area of mental health:

TRUTH:

His death, burial and resurrection makes a way for us to have right standing before God

The crux of the matter

I came to faith at a time when common evangelistic methods included the use of gospel tracts which summarised the main points of the salvation message in easy-to-understand language, often illustrated by helpful diagrams. I myself would have used material such as Billy Graham's *Steps to peace with God* and Campus Crusade's *The four spiritual laws*. I tried to master the contents so that I would be able to present the redemption story to others in the following way:

1. God loves man and wants to have a close relationship with him (Jn. 3:16; 1 Tim. 2:4)

2. Because of his sin, man is separated from a holy God and stands under judgement from Him (Rom. 3:23; 6:23)

3. Jesus came to take the punishment for our sins and meet the righteous standards that God has set (thereby being faithful to His character in terms of appropriately judging sin but also drawing man to Himself in love; Rom. 5:8; 2 Cor. 5:21)

4. As we repent and believe (i.e. put our trust in Him to achieve this on our behalf), the way is made for us to be forgiven and enter into an eternal relationship with God (Jn. 1:12; Rom. 5:1)

Now, this still works for me and I believe that the essential message of the gospel is captured in those four points. However, this presentation of the good news is individually-centred and we need to very much keep in mind that God's plan of salvation is not just personal but involves the vastly bigger picture of the redemption of all creation. Matt Chandler helps us to understand this in his book, *The explicit gospel*, where he talks about the personal aspect of the message (the 'gospel on the ground') and the bigger picture of what God is doing in the world (the 'gospel in the air').

Furthermore, we must guard against reducing genuine faith simply to the utterance of a 'sinner's prayer'; a person's coming to faith involves the preparatory work of the Holy Spirit in that person's heart, a real conviction of sin and a sense of brokenness, a response of faith based on a clear understanding of what the Bible teaches regarding the person and work of Jesus Christ, and an ongoing life of repentance, faith, surrender and obedience, all energised by the grace of God. There is no 'easy believism' involved in true conversion.

The double blessing

Looking more closely at the two key aspects of what Jesus' work on the cross has accomplished:

1) 'Substitutionary atonement'

Jesus stood in our place of judgement such that God's wrath can be satisfied and at the same time His love towards us can be manifested through a restored relationship (some have said that atonement can be read as 'at-one-ment' i.e. two parties being at one through appropriate reconciliation). Another theological term, 'propitiation', can be used i.e. a turning away of God's wrath through an offering by another.

I am thankful to C. J. Mahaney for the following illustration which, although mainly played out in the human dimension, gives us a glimpse of what it means to sacrifice oneself for the sake of many others:

'All die!'

In World War II, Ernest Gordon was a British captive in a Japanese prison camp by the River Kwai in Burma, where the POWs were forced to build a 'railroad of death' for transporting Japanese troops to the battlefront. They were tortured, starved, and worked to the point of exhaustion. Nearly 16,000 died.

Gordon survived the horrors of that experience and wrote about it in a monumental work, Through the Valley of the Kwai, published in 1962 (and later made into the movie To End All Wars). He describes one occasion when, at the end of a workday, the tools were being counted before the prisoners returned to their quarters. A guard declared that a shovel was missing. He began to rant and rave, demanding to know which prisoner had stolen it.

Working himself into a paranoid fury, he ordered whoever was guilty to step forward and take his punishment. No one did. 'All die!' the guard shrieked, 'All die!' He cocked his rifle and aimed it at the prisoners.

At that moment, one man stepped forward. Standing at attention he calmly declared, 'I did it'. The Japanese guard at once clubbed the prisoner to death.

As his friends carried away his lifeless body, the shovels in the tool shed were recounted – only to reveal that there was no missing shovel.[2]

(There is of course only a limit to what this illustration can convey; it is very hard to find a satisfactory analogy for an event which really has no parallel in human history, and which will never be repeated again i.e. the once-for-all death of the Son of God for sinful man.)

2) 'Imputed righteousness'

Not only did Jesus take the punishment for our sins which enables us to be forgiven, He was the only person who ever lived who through His sinless life could fully meet the righteous standards of God Himself. And this righteousness is imputed to us (given to us and treated as if it was ours, through faith) such that when God looks at us, He sees the righteousness of Christ that has been given to us, which forms the basis of His thorough acceptance of us; we become clothed in new robes of righteousness.

2 Cor. 5:21:

> *For He made Him who knew no sin to be sin for us, that we might become the righteousness of God in Him.*

Is. 61:10:

> *I will greatly rejoice in the Lord,*
> *My soul shall be joyful in my God;*
> *For He has clothed me with the garments of salvation,*
> *He has covered me with the robe of righteousness,*
> *As a bridegroom decks himself with ornaments,*
> *And as a bride adorns herself with her jewels.*

We have thus been talking about justification i.e. how sinful man can be made right in the sight of a holy God. It is this question that lies behind a lot of man's search for inner peace. At the risk of oversimplification, some have said that being 'justified' is like:

> *'Just-as-if-I'd never sinned,*
> *Just-as-if-I'd always obeyed.'*

This is utterly radical

1 Cor. 1:18-20:

For the message of the cross is foolishness to those who are perishing, but to us who are being saved it is the power of God. For it is written:
"I will destroy the wisdom of the wise,
And bring to nothing the understanding of the prudent."
Where is the wise? Where is the scribe? Where is the disputer of this age? Has not God made foolish the wisdom of this world?

This method of salvation strikes at the very core of our pride and self-righteousness. It jars against our deeply ingrained need-to-do-it-myself mentality. God grants redemption as a free gift to be received but we would rather try and earn it ourselves through good works that we have done ('justification by works' being a term for this). God's way of salvation goes against the values of this world where self-made success and the achieving of power and status are the aims. But the cross brings us to the end of ourselves and shows us a different path – the way of brokenness and weakness whereby we find truth and power in Christ.

The unbelieving world will laugh at the Saviour who died a gruesome criminal's death, and at His followers who appear so helpless in themselves. But this is again where Christianity is unique. It is based on the supreme self-sacrifice, that of God's only Son, which was the only righteous solution to the pervasiveness of sin. Through this seemingly tragic failure of mission (as it appears to the blinded eye) was birthed a revolution of grace and love that would spread throughout the earth and down the generations for all time.

APPLICATION:

In Christ, we can have acceptance before performance

Acceptance before performance

A key distinctive of the Christian faith when considered alongside all other philosophies and religions is that in Christianity, the way to God is based on what He has already done for us and not on what we need to do for Him. In Christ, we can freely receive His gift of salvation; all He asks of us is a genuine response of repentance and faith, which He enables us to have.

The gospel of Jesus Christ is a message of grace – **G**od's **R**iches **A**t **C**hrist's **E**xpense. Grace is undeserved favour; the more we realise how much we need grace in our lives, the more we can experience the reality of His work on our behalf. It is not that we can thus do whatever we like; rather, the experience of grace truly empowers us to live as God desires. In other words, grace means that we are not saved *by* good works (as if our merit depended on them) but *for* good works (in order to serve others in love; Gal. 5:13).

In short: through faith in Christ, we are granted divine acceptance without having to earn it through human achievement; this spells the end of performance-based living that leads to a drivenness to achieve in order to be affirmed.

The occasion of the baptism of Jesus described in Matt. 3:16-17 has been very instructive to me:

> *When He had been baptized, Jesus came up immediately from the water; and behold, the heavens were opened to Him, and He saw the Spirit of God descending like a dove and alighting upon Him. And suddenly a voice came from heaven, saying, "This is My beloved Son, in whom I am well pleased."*

The sequence of events is worth noting, and is most encouraging. The Son of God received empowering and affirmation from His Father even before He had begun His public ministry, preached any sermons, healed any of the sick, performed any miracles. God was well pleased with Jesus because He was His Son. The Father's pleasure in the Son then became a basis and foundation for His impending mission. Divine acceptance was manifest before any performance was accomplished, and became the starting point for significant service.

Consider also a modern-day parable:

Socks

A young lady kept house for a wealthy executive. She did her work diligently; the property was constantly immaculate. There was one thing though that she struggled greatly with – washing the man's socks. (Memories of childhood would flood her mind whenever she was engaged in this task – her own father had been cruel and abusive; whenever as a young girl she tried to verbally protest he would stuff a dirty sock in her mouth.)

Nevertheless, she made herself do it. In her mind, if she did not, her employer would be thoroughly displeased and terminate her much-needed contract.

As does happen, time and regular contact (he worked from home a lot) led to the sparking of mutual romantic interest and sooner rather than later this progressed into a serious long-term relationship. Marriage ensued and with it a change of status for the woman – no longer a servant whose job security depended on her performance; there were now equal rights, lifelong emotional commitment, a large joint bank account. Socks could have been sent to the cleaners, or even left unwashed, without affecting her place within the home.

But the change in her position was crucial: from a starting place of acceptance and security, the despised activity was no longer a dreaded chore, but an expression of affection and gratitude.

His socks were now being happily washed out of a love that came from being loved. The effect of the past was significantly diminished; grace had overcome fear.

Two potentially helpful applications

This concept can have important applications to some common mental health difficulties. I focus on two areas:

1) <u>Low self-esteem</u>

Self-esteem refers to the way a person views themselves, in their totality. It involves firmly held thoughts, beliefs and feelings and can impact on every area of life and functioning. A person with low self-esteem will have an unhealthily negative view of themselves and draw conclusions about their own worth which are not necessarily based on a fair and realistic appraisal of who they are.

A humanistic approach to this problem would be to try and develop a more balanced self-view i.e. to attempt to find and focus on the good that lies within, and to continue working on those areas where weaknesses reside. It would be about learning not to be too hard on oneself and allowing positive aspects of one's life to be given more acknowledgement and credence.

A potential limitation of tackling the issue this way is that it primarily involves looking within, and what can be produced from the self. People with low self-esteem often honestly cannot see and feel anything worthy within them, and are painfully aware that trying harder to come up with something better to focus on is much more difficult than they had realised.

A follower of Christ has the option of taking a different approach to the challenge of low self-esteem. By contrast, a Christian could come to see that their feelings of unworthiness and inadequacy might actually be a revelation of the truth that in God's sight, apart from Christ, they stand in a place of desperate need, and that the influence of sin and this fallen world goes much deeper than it first appears. So, to begin with, there isn't a fight against the reality of their lack but rather a humble acceptance that the starting point of grace is inner brokenness.

The believer is then not left to wallow in introspective self-deprecation – their accurate appraisal of the cause of their damaged self-esteem is the very thing that drives them to the foot of the cross where they find both liberating forgiveness and the empowering righteousness of another. So, rather than trying to produce some goodness of their own in an attempt to feel less unworthy, they are able to exchange their inadequacy for Christ's perfect adequacy; the pain of low self-esteem can be transformed into the joy of belonging to and becoming like Christ. This process could be summarised as moving from self-esteem to Christ-esteem.

When it comes to developing a healthier sense of self, it can be helpful to meditate on the new identity that we assume whenever we are joined with Christ and become part of His family. Several things about us change fundamentally as a result of our position in Christ and these can powerfully alter the way we view who we are as human beings. I have included a list of these truths in the endnotes[3].

2) Perfectionism

One definition of perfectionism is: the pursuit of acceptance and approval through self-driven achievement, both internal and external.

It often goes hand-in-hand with low self-esteem; someone who feels inferior, insignificant, unlovable, can very easily embark on a lifelong project to be as perfect as possible (in the process setting standards for themselves which are unrealistically demanding) in order to feel some measure of acceptance from others and themselves.

But it is never enough; whenever our acceptance is intrinsically tied in with our performance, it will never be sufficient because we will never reach perfection in and of ourselves.

A revolution of the heart and mind occurs when a Christian realises that all the demands for perfection have already been met by the sinless Saviour who calls us to partake of His own perfect righteousness. We no longer need to strive to perform well enough in order to be accepted; out of a starting position of acceptance through Christ, we are free to perform as best as we can with new motivation and power.

We are thus free to pursue excellence (i.e. from a starting point of acceptance, doing the best we can with the grace He provides) and leave perfectionism (i.e. trying to meet unrealistic demands in our own limited ability in order to gain approval) behind.

The parable of the talents found in Matt. 25:14-30 is one of my favourite illustrations in the Bible. It shows us that our call is to faithfulness and not merely quantitative productivity. The servants who were given less but were faithful with what they had been provided with received the same reward as those who were given more at the start. Knowing this can really help us avoid the deadly comparison trap that we can easily fall into if we are in any way insecure about who are in Christ. Our task is to be fully committed where we are, with what we have, and to leave the results of our labour up to Him.

'Good enough for now'

There is a remarkably practical and emotionally experiential upshot to all of this: I call it being able to be 'good enough for now', which I think has at least 2 components:

1) 'Total acceptance'

If you think about it this is quite marvellous: we can actually live with a sense of acceptance and approval each and every moment of our lives, simply because our intrinsic worth depends upon what Jesus has already done for us, and not what we still need to do for Him. There is a godly contentment that is possible in whatever situation we find ourselves in, as we do all things through Christ who strengthens us (Phil. 4:11-13).

This of course does not mean that we are remaining stagnant in the spiritual life but rather we have a secure base, a calm and alert poise, that can facilitate Spirit-empowered change. It does mean that we are not living from one moment to the next constantly wondering if we have learnt enough and done enough to be able to rest for a while.

2) 'I'm doing well'

Having the righteousness of Christ by faith by definition means that I am, because of Him, pleasing in God's sight and that His standards are being met on my behalf. If I am applying myself faithfully and doing my best I can honestly say that I'm doing well in whatever it is I am doing, regardless of how things turn out by way of outcome or results.

It is not that I am just barely doing enough to force a slight, reluctant nod of approval from a hard-to-please Heavenly Father, I am actually doing very well when I am walking by faith in Christ. Everything I do can become precious gifts of service even though by the world's standards, the tasks may seem small and insignificant.

It goes without saying that maintaining this kind of peace-filled spirit does depend on responding appropriately to the conviction of sin and disobedience. We cannot neglect to immediately deal with the sting of a seared conscience, or seek to quickly repair if possible a relationship fracture that will stand in the way of interpersonal harmony.

TRUTH:

We are adopted into the family of God

God thinks bigger than just individuals

One of the dangers of a self-serving, consumer society is that it can breed individualism, where people think mainly about how things impact their own lives and there is a loss of the connectedness between persons that is required to create healthy, thriving communities.

Christians too can come to think of the spiritual life as being primarily an individual pursuit, with an overemphasis on individual, personal growth. This is antithetical to how the Bible describes discipleship, as that which should be occurring collectively within the body of Christ. The epistles were written to groups of believers; the prayer that the Lord instructed us to pray begins with '*Our* Father in heaven...' and goes on to use *us* several times rather than *me* (Matt. 6:9-13).

God is in the process of building a holy nation, His own special people (1 Pet. 2:9), not just separate persons disconnected from each other. He has a vision for a blessed community of the redeemed that will reflect His glory. I once heard a preacher explain the reason, in his opinion, that God created man: "God had such joy and satisfaction within the relationships of the Trinity that He wanted to extend His family for all eternity."

We become His children

When we come to faith in Christ, we are adopted into His very own family, and become His children (Eph. 1:4-5; 1 Jn. 3:1-2). We move from being enemies of God, dead in our trespasses, to being recipients of His grace. We are not just acquaintances of God, or even friends – we are family; not just tolerated or put up with in the sense of being barely accepted but valued and cherished vastly more than a human being loves his own family.

Having received the Spirit of adoption, we can now relate to Him as our Heavenly Father. Rom. 8:14-17:

For as many as are led by the Spirit of God, these are sons of God. For you did not receive the spirit of bondage again to fear, but you received the Spirit of adoption by whom we cry out, "Abba, Father." The Spirit Himself bears witness with our spirit that we are children of God, and if children, then heirs – heirs of God and joint heirs with Christ, if indeed we suffer with Him, that we may also be glorified together.

Consider the following compilation of Scripture that someone has put together as 'The Father's Love Letter':

My Child,

You may not know about Me, but I know everything about you (Ps. 139:1). I know when you sit down and when you rise up (Ps. 139:2). I am familiar with all your ways (Ps. 139:3). Even the very hairs on your head are numbered (Matt. 10:29-31). For you were made in My image (Gen. 1:27). In Me you live and move and have your being (Acts 17:28). For you are My offspring (Acts 17:28). I knew you even before you were conceived (Jer. 1:4-5). I chose you when I planned creation (Eph. 1:11-12). You were not a mistake, for all your days are written in my book (Ps. 139:15-16). I determined the exact time of your birth and where you would live (Acts 17:26). You are fearfully and wonderfully made (Ps. 139:14). I knit you together in your mother's womb (Ps. 139:13). And brought you forth on the day you were born (Ps. 71:6). I have been misrepresented by those who don't know Me (Jn. 8:41-44). I am not distant and angry, but am the complete expression of love (1 Jn. 4:16). And it is my desire to lavish My love on you (1 Jn. 3:1). Simply because you are My child and I am your Father (1 Jn. 3:1). I offer you more than your earthly father ever could (Matt. 7:11). For I am the perfect Father (Matt. 5:48). Every good gift that you receive comes from My hand (Js. 1:17). For I am your provider and I meet all your needs (Matt. 6:31-33). My plan for your future has always been filled with hope (Jer. 29:11). Because I love you with an everlasting love (Jer. 31:3). My thoughts toward you are countless as the sand on the seashore (Ps. 139:17-18). And I rejoice over you with singing (Zeph. 3:17). I will never stop doing good to you (Jer. 32:40). For you are My treasured possession (Ex. 19:5). I desire to establish you with all my heart and all my soul (Jer. 32:41). And I want to show you great and marvellous things (Jer. 33:3). If you seek Me with all your heart, you will find Me (Deut. 4:29). Delight in Me and I will give you the desires of your heart (Ps. 37:4). For it is I who gave you those desires (Phil. 2:13). I am able to do more for you than you could possibly imagine (Eph. 3:20). For I am your greatest encourager (2 Thess. 2:16-17). I am also the Father who comforts you in all your troubles (2 Cor. 1:3-4). When you are brokenhearted, I am close to you (Ps. 34:18). As a shepherd carries a lamb, I have carried you close to My heart (Is. 40:11). One day I will wipe away every tear from your eyes (Rev. 21:3-4). And I'll take away all the pain you have suffered on this earth (Rev. 21:3-4). I am your Father, and I love you even as I love My son, Jesus (Jn. 17:23). For in Jesus, my love for you is revealed (Jn. 17:26). He is the exact representation of My being (Heb. 1:3). He came to demonstrate that I am for you, not against you (Rom. 8:31). And to tell you that I am not counting your sins (2 Cor. 5:18-19). Jesus died so that you and I could be reconciled (2 Cor. 5:18-19). His death was the ultimate expression of My love for you (1 Jn. 4:10). I gave up everything I loved that I might gain your love (Rom. 8:31-32). If you receive the gift of my son Jesus, you receive Me (1 Jn. 2:23). And nothing will ever separate you from My love again (Rom. 8:38-39). Come home and I'll throw the biggest party heaven has ever seen (Lk. 15:7). I have always been Father, and will always be Father (Eph. 3:14-15). My question is... Will you be My child (Jn. 1:12-13)? I am waiting for you (Lk. 15:11-32).

Love,

Your Dad
Almighty God[4]

The church becomes our family

When we become part of His body, the fellowship of believers becomes our new family. By His love and power, the relationships formed within this new community can bring healing and restoration to troubled souls looking for a place to belong and be nurtured.

The reality of God's new family will hopefully not just be a theoretical nicety but a practical outworking of His love shed upon the hearts of His people. In the midst of societal bonds being broken, marriages crumbling and families being torn apart, the church has the potential to rise up and be a Christ-centred family which welcomes the lost and loves them as brothers and sisters, sons and daughters. The hungry can be fed, the homeless given shelter, the lonely can be embraced.

This is good news for those who have no real home. Ps. 68:4-6:

> *Sing to God, sing praises to His name;*
> *Extol Him who rides on the clouds,*
> *By His name YAH,*
> *And rejoice before Him.*
> *A father of the fatherless, a defender of widows,*
> *Is God in His holy habitation.*
> *God sets the solitary in families;*
> *He brings out those who are bound into prosperity;*
> *But the rebellious dwell in a dry land.*

APPLICATION:

We can experience the blessings of a new family in Christ

The impact of families on our upbringing

Our families, specifically the kind of upbringing and experiences we have within our family context, are a major influence on how we develop as human beings in all areas of life. God has ordained the family to be a vehicle through which the love and nurture of God Himself can be expressed, such that growing individuals will have a stable foundation for their progression into adulthood, and be able to project this positive cycle into the subsequent generations.

'Attachment theory' is an important concept in modern psychotherapeutic practice. We have come to clearly see that the quality of the relationship with the primary care giver in the early stages of life has a crucial influence on the psychological and emotional development of the individual. Some models of psychological therapy have as their basis the goal of providing a corrective attachment experience to those who have been very damaged in early life.

The reality is of course that many, many people have not had a good enough family environment, either past or present. The imperfections and shortcomings of mankind can show up starkly within the proximity of family relationships. Many problems can arise, often passed down from one generation to another.

On the one hand, abusive, neglectful parenting can leave traumatic psychological scars that subsequently require lengthy emotional healing. On the other, overly critical and protective parenting can foster anxiety, low self-esteem and perfectionism. People can learn all sorts of unhealthy patterns from their families (without even realising it) e.g. impatience, fear and anger in the face of conflict or an avoidance of openly discussing difficult thoughts and feelings, let alone being able to work through them.

The good news is that when the church is functioning as it should, it can become an organic, thriving repository of healthy interpersonal relationships which can be accessed by those who have previously been deprived of these.

The church can come into its own in this area

I believe that this is where the church can come into its own. In the area of family life, the people of God can not only bring crucial truth and perspective on how families can be helped, they can actually provide new and different experiences of family.

Within the church, there are potential fathers and mothers, brothers and sisters who can provide a new and different family experience for those who have come from broken and dysfunctional families. Within this atmosphere, the goodness and love of God can be modelled and shared in ways that contribute to the formation of more integrated and whole human beings.

Where else can people find this kind of lifelong loving community? Mental health services, which often become a default caring environment for isolated and vulnerable individuals, are overstretched trying to provide sufficient continuity of care when longer-term supportive input is required; it is time for the church to rise up and take responsibility for being the kind of family that people are in desperate need of.

The beauty here is that, with God's help, everyone can participate. You don't need special skills or training to be family if you have the right heart attitude and willingness to serve. We don't just need more professional counsellors but more mothers who will cook wholesome meals for the hungry, fathers who will take the lonely and isolated to sports matches, siblings who will just spend time doing fun things with people who feel as if they don't fit in with anyone. Everyone touched by Christ personally and by His vision for corporate renewal can play a part in this.

In the biblical counselling book, *How people change*, Chapter 5: 'Change is a community project', the authors present a powerful description of life and growth within the context of God's family, arguing that such transformation can happen in no other setting.[5] It reminded me of the African proverb, 'it takes a village to raise a child', which I think can be adapted to 'it takes a church family to disciple a Christian.'

A reality check

I realise that I write in aspirational tones. I am aware that too many people have been hurt within the context of church relationships. The body of Christ has a lot to do to become a strong, welcoming family for the fatherless and motherless, and to mobilise its resources to actually be the very representation of Christ to those yearning for a place to truly belong.

And yet we cannot get away from the inspiring example of the dynamic early church community (Acts 2:41-47; 4:32-35) and the challenge in Jn. 13:34-35:

> *"A new commandment I give to you, that you love one another; as I have loved you, that you also love one another. By this all will know that you are My disciples, if you have love for one another."*

If we can get our act together and by the grace of God be the family of God that He intended, the witness to the world will be immense, and the opportunity to draw people into a community of love and grace will be ever present.

TRUTH:

We have a model of true forgiveness

Jesus provides the supreme example

Some have said that forgiveness is the defining mark of Christianity. I think it is one of several outstanding distinctives of the way of Christ, alongside salvation by grace through faith, the spiritual reality of new birth, progressive sanctification by the power of the Spirit etc.

There is no doubt that forgiveness is at the centre of our reconciliation with God, an epitome of grace. Our faith is based upon the fact that we can and have been forgiven, even though in and of ourselves we do not deserve it, entirely through the kindness and mercy of God who has provided a way for sin to be judged through the sacrificial death of His Son. Rom. 4:7-8 (quoting Ps. 32:1-2):

> "Blessed are those whose lawless deeds are forgiven,
> And whose sins are covered;
> Blessed is the man to whom the Lord shall not impute sin."

Jesus provides us with the great example of God's forgiveness. He bore the sins of the whole world such that forgiveness could be provided for transgressions past, present and future. He not only made the way for us to be forgiven, but set in place a standard of forgiveness for others which if adhered to can bring much blessing to all parties concerned.

An analysis of forgiveness

Forgiveness involves several aspects:

- To grant pardon for a fault or an offense
- To free from the obligation of payment (e.g. of a debt)
- To cease to feel resentment or malice towards the offender
- To choose not to bring the matter up again if the issue has been resolved

When preceded by genuine repentance on the part of the offender, forgiveness opens the door for godly reconciliation where this is appropriate and necessary. It allows for the creation of new redemptive opportunities, the salvation of souls. As one speaker put it: 'Forgiveness is the gift of a new future.'[6]

Three important points:

1) <u>Forgiveness does not mean we don't hurt deeply</u>

When there has been a significant transgression, it would be an utter mistake to expect forgiveness to come without allowing the offended person to honestly feel and express their hurt and pain. To do so would be to deny their humanity and deprive them of the necessary period of grief and cathartic healing before they can reach a place of considering true forgiveness. When somebody is trying to process extreme hurt, the people of God need to come around and alongside, to hold and support and listen with the heart of compassionate patience.

2) Forgiveness is not cheap

Forgiveness is not cheap because sin is serious. Our forgiveness by God is not 'free' – it cost the life of His only Son. It did not come to us automatically; through a Spirit-inspired process of revelation and conviction, we are enabled to see how far short we fall from God's standards and how we regularly miss the mark and as we respond in repentance and faith, His forgiveness then becomes a reality.

It is my view that for serious offences, there can be no true forgiveness (certainly not the kind that leads to meaningful reconciliation) without genuine repentance in the heart of the offender[7]. This does not mean that the offended party should be paralysed by unresolved trauma in the absence of this; they are still free to pursue their own journey of emotional healing which will include eventually releasing anger, bitterness and demand for justice, ultimately surrendering the matter to God Himself.

3) Within the context of God's grace, forgiveness is to be freely given

For serious offences, if there is a demonstration of genuine repentance and the specific asking for forgiveness, there is a clear imperative for us to forgive from the heart, empowered by the very grace of God Himself. This may be much more than a one-off affair but rather a gradual and often painful process; nevertheless, that is our call in Christ and the rewards of doing this both for now (lasting peace of mind) and for all eternity (the redemption of lost souls) are not insignificant.

For minor offenses, and for regular conflicts, misunderstandings, letting downs etc. that we all experience day in day out, a general attitude of grace and forgiveness is called for, a walking in love which involves among other things longsuffering, kindness, forbearance etc. (1 Cor. 13:4-8).

I believe that a lot of the less serious hurt that we experience as part of living in a fallen world full of imperfect people can be dealt with through the rubric of 'love covers a multitude of sins' (1 Pet. 4:8).

In addition, David Benner helps us with a further understanding of what forgiveness is not[8]:

- To forgive is not to forget (but to be able to remember without resentment or malice)
- To forgive is not to excuse (but to see the offence for the sin that it is, which is why forgiveness is required in the first place)
- To forgive is not to ignore (but to face the reality of the widespread impact of the offence)
- To forgive is not necessarily to extend unconditional trust (but to be wise in considering whether it would be safe and sensible to allow another chance for relational contact)

He calls and enables us to walk in forgiveness

His forgiveness of us is the basis for our forgiveness of others. When we struggle to forgive, He supplies the grace to do so by helping us acknowledge how much we ourselves have been undeservingly forgiven. Incorporating the vertical dimension is crucial in having a biblical approach to forgiveness. Sinful behaviour by us and towards us does not just have horizontal ramifications; the greater sin is against God Himself.

We are taught (in Matt. 5:23-24) that reconciliation is required before worship. Unforgiveness blocks the flow of relationship in and out of your soul. Anyone who is married I'm sure has experienced those awful periods of (mutual) silent treatment, when communication has broken down between spouses and feelings of anger/injustice are churning – we soon come to learn that breakthrough is curtailed until forgiveness takes place, on both sides.

In the Lord's Prayer (Matt. 6:9-15), we are instructed to ask God to 'forgive us our debts, as we forgive our debtors' (v12) and that 'if you forgive men their trespasses, your heavenly Father will also forgive you. But if you do not forgive men their trespasses, neither will your Father forgive your trespasses.' (v14-15).

Matt. 18:21-35 describes the parable of the unforgiving servant who incurred the wrath of his master when, after having been graciously forgiven a vast debt, refused to release a debtor who owed him a miniscule sum in comparison.

A word of caution: whilst we are commanded to freely forgive, we need also to ensure that our offer of forgiveness is not superficial and in some situations is withheld unless preceded by genuine repentance.

A murderer who has shown no remorse continues to stand under the judgement of those he has hurt.

On the side of those who have suffered, in the face of unrepentance (and of course even when remorse has been shown), there is work to be done emotionally to ensure that they themselves do not allow justified anger to progress to stifling bitterness and resentment – but this in my opinion is more of a 'letting go' rather than forgiveness of the other person in the true sense[9].

For those who have been severely violated, there is great comfort in knowing that, in addition to having to face the full force of the law, the perpetrator will be subject to the divine justice of God in due course.

APPLICATION:

We can live in the freedom that forgiveness brings

We have the power to forgive

Christianity is not a religion of lists and rules which we need to try and keep to the best of our abilities. It is profound inner change by the Spirit of God that empowers us to become more and more like Christ Himself.

In the area of forgiveness, we not only have the imperative to forgive but the inspiration to do so, as He enables us to. We have not only a new desire to bring about reconciliation through acts of forgiveness, but the basis and ability to carry it out in practice.

This does not mean that it is always easy. Forgiveness can be the hardest thing for someone to do, particularly if the hurt has been deep and prolonged. In those cases, forgiveness becomes more like a gradual process than a one-off event. There is much faith-led and deliberate choice on our part to decide to forgive when everything else within us cries out for retribution.

Some key applications to mental health/wellbeing

When the grace to walk in true forgiveness is present, the potential benefits for a believer's mental health are very significant:

1) There is more ability to deal effectively with the past

Forgiveness is one key that can help us gain a new perspective on past events that have caused hurt, disappointment and regret. Without denying that those things happened, and with proper emotional expression and relational support, forgiveness provides a way in which the chains of bitterness and resentment can be broken, paving the way for greater degrees of emotional freedom.

2) There is an answer to guilt and shame

Guilt involves an awareness that something wrong has been done (real or imagined). Shame is a distressing feeling that arises in relation to how we think we appear to others (not always related to what we have done). They of course often go hand-in-hand. So many people are weighed down by a burden of guilt and/or shame which prevents them from living with the freedom of self-contentment and the ability to relate effectively with others.

The fact that even at our worst, Christ died for us (Rom. 5:8), provides assurance that guilt and shame need not gain a foothold in our lives, for God Himself has forgiven and is actively at work to restore and transform us from glory to glory (2 Cor. 3:18). We no longer need to find absolution and intrinsic worth from within ourselves – such has been given to us through what Jesus has done on the cross in reconciling God and man.

3) There is a way to restore broken relationships, to the glory of God

In many cases, though unfortunately not in all as the full restoration of relationships requires serious effort from both sides which is not always forthcoming, the process of forgiveness can lead to the mending of broken relationships, even those where there has been a rift for many years.

In these situations, forgiveness is not just an intellectual, transactional exercise – it is the attitude and choice of heart that can usher in the very healing power of God into a circumstance and bring about a posture of divine love where there had previously been anger and hatred. In some cases, with the balm of forgiveness, broken relationships may not only be restored but be brought to a new level of depth and intimacy, in a way that leads onlookers to marvel and give due praise to God.

'Perpetual fresh starts'

On a very practical and day-to-day level, the firm theological basis that Christians can have as regards a forgiveness that is freely available to both receive and give enables us to have what I call 'perpetual fresh starts', an ongoing lifestyle where accounts can be kept short and a lightness of spirit maintained.

In the course of any given day, we don't always walk in the Spirit as we should; we easily step into living by our own strength, becoming annoyed when things don't go our way, getting offended by the insensitivity of others, accumulating a whole range of experiences which steal our inner peace and adversely affect our relationship with God and others.

In Christ, this temporary distance from the sustaining presence of God can be rectified quickly through acknowledgement of how we have strayed from His will, repentance for slipping into self-reliance and a thankful turning again to the grace and mercy of God. Following our honest and humble response, the experience of forgiveness can come straight away because the saving work of Christ on the cross can become gloriously effective in that very moment. There is no more condemnation. We are free to approach the throne of grace in confidence, to be filled again with His Holy Spirit and continue on the path of sanctification. We can start afresh, over and over again, with unlimited attempts.

This means that we can truly 'live light', carrying few burdens (e.g. of guilt, shame, unresolved anger, regret etc.) with us as we journey through life, seeking to do His will in all things. We can actually and experientially 'let go'; we also can forgive ourselves knowing that God Himself holds no offence against us because of the sacrifice of Christ on our behalf which we have gratefully appropriated for ourselves. Now, if this isn't great news I don't know what is!

Chapter 5

POWER TO CHANGE

Real power to change is available to the faithful believer in Christ.

At a personal level, the gospel is about the transformation of self-dependent, sinful human beings into God-reliant, increasingly mature followers of Christ. When it comes to any change, not least that which involves the shaping of character and values, the problem is often not one of ignorance as regards what needs to be achieved; the real challenge is how to find the ability to actually do what needs to be done.

In the plan of God revealed through the gospel, He has made a way for His people to be empowered for transformation, through the indwelling Holy Spirit whose ever present help in our lives has been made possible through the death, burial, resurrection and ascension of Jesus Christ.

This has often struck me as the great blessing of the gospel: that Christ died not just for the forgiveness of our sins, but to make a way for the Holy Spirit to dwell within us and be the very source of our life in God. God has not just appointed us for His purposes, He has anointed us by His Spirit such that those purposes can be fulfilled.

Consider the following truths of the gospel and their potential applications to the area of mental health:

TRUTH:

The Holy Spirit indwells and empowers us

General introduction to the Holy Spirit

The Holy Spirit, a person not an 'it' or an impersonal force, is part of the triune God, equal in power and authority and active in the gospel plan of God since the beginning of creation (Gen. 1:2).

He is often misunderstood and, sadly, unnecessarily feared by those who have not been well taught about who He is and what He does. On the one hand, there are those who wrongly claim some ecstatic emotional experiences as being the movement of God's Spirit; on the other, whole groups of believers are missing out on the dynamic power of the Holy Spirit for everyday life and ministry.

Early in my Christian life, I was fortunate to have been brought into a church that valued both the Word and the Spirit of God. Solid biblical teaching was complemented by healthy expression of spiritual gifts. Our previous pastor used to say, "The Word alone, and we dry up; the Spirit alone, we blow up; the Word and Spirit together we grow up (and when Jesus comes again we go up!)"

Brief survey of the Holy Spirit in the Old and New Testaments

The presence and work of the Holy Spirit can be found in the Bible from cover to cover.

Throughout the Old Testament, before the redemptive work of Christ on the cross was completed, the Holy Spirit would be at work in individuals in a specific and temporary way in order to empower them for the tasks that God had called them to. The Spirit's presence was recognised in a number of the Lord's servants e.g. Joseph (Gen. 41:38), Joshua (Num. 27:18) and Daniel (Dan. 5:11-14). The Spirit came upon certain people at particular times e.g. Balaam (Num. 24:2), Gideon (Judges 6:34), Samson (Judges 14:6), Saul (1 Sam. 11:6), David (1 Sam. 16:13) and Elijah (1 Kgs. 18:46). Bezalel was filled with the Spirit for the express task of assisting with the building of God's tabernacle (Ex. 31:3).

In the New Testament, following the incarnation of a Saviour who would bear the sins of the world, the Holy Spirit would come to indwell believers in a more global and permanent sense (Jn. 14:16; 1 Cor. 3:16; 6:19); this would lead to a life of continually being filled with the Spirit, walking daily in His power (Gal. 2:20; 5:16; Eph. 5:18). The Holy Spirit has been given to us as a Helper, Comforter, Counsellor, who leads us into all truth, empowers us for service and glorifies Jesus (Jn. 14:16-17; 16:13-14; Acts. 1:8).

The experience of the Holy Spirit for present day believers

I find it helpful to think of our relationship and experiences of the Holy Spirit in the following ways:

- <u>Born of the Spirit</u>: the God-initiated regeneration of the human spirit by the Holy Spirit that enables us to respond in faith to His grace (Jn. 3:1-8; Tit. 3:5; 1 Pet. 1:23 etc.)

- <u>Baptised with the Spirit</u>: an initial infilling of the Holy Spirit that brings us into community within the body of Christ (Acts 1:5; 2:1-4; 1 Cor. 12:13 etc.)

- <u>Filled with the Spirit</u>: the experience of surrendering to Him and allowing Him to have full control of our lives that His presence may be manifested in and through us in an ongoing way (Acts 4:31; 6:3; Eph. 5:18 etc.)

- <u>Led by the Spirit/walking in the Spirit</u>: the empowering of the Spirit for everyday, moment-by-moment obedience to His leading and guidance which help us to grow in sanctification and fulfil His will (Rom. 8:1, 14; Gal. 5:16; Col. 3:15-16 etc.)

- <u>Fruit of the Spirit</u>: the manifestation of the very character of Christ in and through us as we allow our thoughts, feeling and behaviours to be shaped and directed by His Spirit (Jn. 15:1-5; Gal. 5:22-23; Eph. 5:8-11 etc.)

- <u>Gifts of the Spirit</u>: supernatural abilities as given by the Spirit for the specific purpose of building up the body of Christ and empowering the church for its tasks of evangelism and discipleship (Rom. 12:6-8; 1 Cor. 12:1-11; Eph. 4:11-16 etc.)

- <u>Ministering in the power of the Spirit</u>: moving out in service to the Lord and mission to the world in His power, with signs and wonders accompanying (Mk. 16:15-18; Acts 3:1-10; 4:29-30 etc.)

We should note that the Holy Spirit doesn't overpower and control us as if we were puppets. Rather, He becomes joined with our spirits creating an inner union with Him out of which His life flows. We need to cooperate with Him and submit our wills to His such that the Holy Spirit can have full freedom to guide our very thoughts and actions.

APPLICATION:

We have a new power to live and change

Fundamental inner change

There are some tremendous implications arising from the reality of the indwelling Holy Spirit in the lives of believers:

1) We have new conviction

We are able to see the folly of self-reliance. There is a sensitivity to sin and a readiness to repent that can come only from the convicting work of the Spirit. There is steadily increasing faith in the sufficiency of Christ for all things pertaining to life and godliness.

2) We have new desires

A hunger and thirst for the things of God is birthed and drives us to pursue the Lord with all our hearts. If the Spirit is truly allowed to work in our lives, there is a growing revulsion of that which is displeasing to Him, and greater love for that which He desires. The passing pleasures of this world are seen as such and pale in comparison with the joy of really abiding in Him; this brings to mind the phrase of Thomas Chalmers: 'The expulsive power of a new affection.'

c) We have new ability

A life of following the Spirit brings wisdom. As we submit our hearts and minds to Him, we gain His perspective on the way things are. We are better able to discern the right course of action in a particular situation. We are able to know the very mind of Christ (1 Cor. 2:16).

A life of abiding in the Christ (John 15) brings strength to follow through on what wisdom has guided us to think, say and do. This can be through the sheer willingness and energy to obey His leading which arises out of a human spirit that has been quickened by His Spirit. It can also come through the formation of right motives e.g. love and service for the sake of the kingdom of God.

It is important to realise that we are talking about vibrant spiritual reality here, not just dry theoretical concepts. Profound changes have taken place at the core of our being, and continue to occur. Romans 6-8 provides a rich theological discourse about the truth and outworking of our inner conversion and renewal.

Divine strategies for issues faced

Knowing that we have the power of the Holy Spirit as a divine resource in the midst of our struggles brings us to a helpful starting point where we can ask the Lord for His guidance about several areas:

1) What is the key issue?

'A problem well-defined is half-solved' is a saying that has stuck in my mind for years. God can put His finger on exactly the issue that He wants us to be seeking transforming grace for, be it attitudes or actions, problems which are at the root of our struggle and not just the superficial presentations.

2) What is the strategy to face it?

'Teach me Your ways' is a favourite prayer of mine which comes to my heart and lips whilst facing a challenging situation. Here we come to God in humble surrender, with expectation that He will graciously provide wisdom and guidance on the most helpful way to approach that particular problem.

3) What is the next thing I need to do, by His strength?

'Do the next right thing' is a maxim that I have found helpful when trying to break down what needs to be done in trying circumstances. Here we seek the Lord for the grace to make one initial change that sets us on our way towards further victory. In this way, the overall task of change can become less overwhelming and may be appropriately tackled on a step-by-step basis.

A particular application to the area of stress and anxiety

I believe that for a Christian, the empowering of the Holy Spirit has a particular application to the area of stress and anxiety, issues that affect almost everyone in modern day society.

In general terms[1], feelings of anxiety arise whenever we perceive that the external pressure or threat that is coming our way is greater than our inner ability to cope with and manage it. We thus feel anxious, fearful and potentially overwhelmed. We try harder to find the strength from within but are defeated and disappointed when we can't muster enough of our own resources.

There is a different path available to the submitted follower of Christ, who is constantly drawing upon the grace of God through the Holy Spirit in all areas and during all occasions of life. There is surely external pressure and threat that will come; what is unique is that the very resources of heaven channelled through His wisdom and strength for the moment is there to be accessed by the faithful believer.

Selwyn Hughes gives this helpful advice:

> *Someone asked a radiant Christian how he managed to keep free from worry. He replied, "I know that God won't let anything come my way that He and I together can't handle."*[2]

As we trust in the Lord with all our hearts and lean not on our own understanding, He will direct our paths (Prov. 3:5-6). As our minds are stayed on Him, He will keep us in perfect peace (Is. 26:3). Anxieties, cares and concerns can be lifted up to the Lord in prayer as and when they occur (Phil. 4:6-7; 1 Pet. 5:7), giving the opportunity for the peace of God to rule in our hearts (Col. 3:15).

The experience of stress and anxiety has a clear biological component. To simplify what are complex neurochemical systems, there is a part of our brain that has the tendency to trigger an emotional response to incoming stimuli a split second before information reaches a different, higher area where it can be processed more rationally.

When we are under pressure, if we are able to take a moment to reflect before we react, to think before we act, we are giving ourselves more opportunity to weigh up the situation more realistically and come up with a more suitable response. In the Christian life, the practices of prayer, meditation on God's Word, waiting upon the Lord etc. can all help us cultivate a more measured and less hurried approach to the stresses that we will inevitably face. Interestingly, the concept of having a more 'mindful' stance when facing life challenges is being increasingly recognised as an efficacious psychotherapeutic principle[3].

TRUTH:

We are called to holiness

What is holiness?

The word 'holiness' can conjure up uncomfortable images of pious people whose apparent godliness seems way beyond the reach of ordinary Christians who struggle with all kinds of sin and suffering. Or, it could bring to mind examples of holier-than-thou individuals whose underlying heart attitudes do not match their outward professions and who seem detached from the reality of life and all its messiness. Sadly, it can sometimes carry such a negative connotation that people think of it as something to be avoided rather than aspired to.

In essence, holiness is about being set apart for God. It is about becoming more and more like Jesus in character and affections and desire to do the will of God. Holiness involves wholeness –

health in spirit, soul and body, all parts of our being becoming integrated and working together for His ultimate glory. It is not a mystical divine state reserved for the spiritual elite but an everyday practical concept that needs to be played out in the nitty-gritty of life.

Holiness can be thought of as both positional and progressive. In one sense, we are made righteous in Christ the moment we trust in and receive His grace; we can be called 'saints' and not just sinners (Acts 9:13; 1 Cor. 1:2; Eph. 4:12). At the same time, we are continually growing in holiness as the Spirit of God moves and works in our lives, transforming us into the image of Christ (Rom. 8:29; 2 Cor. 3:18; Eph. 4:20-24).

The call to holiness

1 Pet. 1:13-16:

> *Therefore gird up the loins of your mind, be sober, and rest your hope fully upon the grace that is to be brought to you at the revelation of Jesus Christ; as obedient children, not conforming yourselves to the former lusts, as in your ignorance; but as He who called you is holy, you also be holy in all your conduct, because it is written, "Be holy, for I am holy."*

We are made in His image (Gen. 1:27) and called to be like Him. It is the *Holy* Spirit who draws, convicts and sanctifies us. As I mentioned in the introduction to this book, God is more interested in our holiness than our happiness.

In the Sermon on the Mount, Jesus taught that blessed are the pure in heart for they shall see God (Matt. 5:8). In Heb. 12:14, the author exhorts us to pursue peace with all people, and holiness, without which no one will see the Lord. It is hard to envisage a higher privilege in life than to 'see God'.

The ability to be holy

When thinking about holiness, there is a danger that we can become discouraged and deflated at the thought of how far we are from reflecting the holiness of God in our lives. We look at others who appear more righteous than us and think that we could never be like them, so what is the point of really trying anyway.

Thankfully, there is good news! As previously described, not only does God call us to a task, He also equips us for it. The Bible describes several overlapping paths towards holiness in everyday life, as described in the next section. These are not just rules to be obeyed but life-giving principles that represent an outflow of the Holy Spirit that is being given full permission to work freely in and through a surrendered heart.

As someone put it, in relation to renewed desires and ability:

> '(In Christ) we have a new want to and a new can do!'

APPLICATION:

We have the privilege of experiencing the joy of holiness

The joy of holiness

It is vital we appreciate the joy that can accompany holiness. This can be so hard to fathom in the highly stimulating, entertainment-saturated, instantly-gratifying society that we live in. Ethical standards have been eroded in the name of freedom, equality and enlightenment. Yet there is no greater joy than being with Him and being like Him, to be 'captured by a greater vision' than that which worldly pleasures can ever provide[4].

We can easily fall into thinking that God's commandments are for our restriction and restraint when actually they represent His grand design for living which, if followed, can bring much freedom, joy and fruitfulness. God does not lay down a standard of righteousness because He is a joyless taskmaster but rather, as Maker of the universe, He knows when and how human beings are going to be functioning at their best and experiencing all the good things that God desires for them.

Holiness is not stuffy, boring, always difficult to live in, impossible to really achieve. A person growing in holiness does not have to be a dour, sullen, tense one. We are not expecting sinless perfection this side of eternity; but we have the privilege of being like Jesus, by His grace, in the moment, continually allowing His life to flow in and through us to produce a greater measure of the character of Christ.

As we pursue holiness in the power of the Spirit, we can come to benefit from the joy of purity which brings a depth of peace, mental wellbeing and spiritual maturity that only a life lived right with and before God can bring.

Pathways to holiness

He makes the way for us to partake of His holiness. The following truths and principles are some ways in which this divine empowering is worked out in the area of sanctification:

1) The power of sin over our lives is broken

Romans 6-8 gives important teaching about the intrinsic change that occurs whenever we move from being ruled by our sinful nature to being controlled by the Spirit. Something is different on the inside; we are no longer slaves to sin. We now have the effective power of choice, to be able to choose righteousness rather than sin (hence becoming slaves to righteousness). So, it is important that we count ourselves as dead to sin but alive to God in Christ Jesus (Rom. 6:11). If not, we will continually believe that we have no power over sin and repeatedly decide not to choose the righteous path.

2) He has provided a pathway of restoration and cleansing

When we do fall into disobedience, He has made a way for us to come back to Him through His conviction of sin, our response of repentance and confession, the asking for and receiving of forgiveness and the forsaking of sin (Prov. 28:13; 32; 38; 51; 1 Jn. 1:9; Js. 5:14, 16 etc.). This gives us the opportunity to promptly deal with sin when it arises or when we fall into it, be restored to a close relationship with God and others and move on steadily with a clear conscience.

This also gives us a way of addressing the kind of genuine guilt that can lead to crushing depression and despair. In this way, the crux of the problem – a troubled spirit secondary to a violation of the ways of God – can be dealt with quickly and effectively because He has provided the path of peace through true forgiveness and reconciliation.

Furthermore, we are able to be utterly honest about our sins, struggles and temptations. before God – just read through the book of Psalms to see a collection of open and raw communications with Him; sometimes heartfelt prayer, admitting our weakness and calling upon the Lord for strength, is what we need more than spiritual analysis or a new method to follow[5].

3) We are given a way of dealing with temptation

Because of the possibility of us choosing to follow fleshly desires, temptation will always be something that believers have to be prepared to contend with this side of heaven. Indeed, in the New Testament, the same Greek word is used for testing and temptation such that in a situation which calls for a heart response, we can react in way that strengthens our faith through testing or weakens it through falling into temptation.

Perhaps God leaves us with the ability to be tempted (but not beyond what we are able to bear; 1 Cor. 10:13) because it is also the opportunity to be tested, to grow deeply, and be proven for His glory. His interest is to strengthen us and develop maturity within us, through loving discipline (Heb. 12:5-7). God's Word empowered by His Spirit provides us with a robust approach to temptation:

a) *Acknowledge the reality of temptation*

Temptation can strike anyone at any time, whether they are in a difficult situation or even if they appear be doing quite well in life. Some would argue that a believer who is pressing into the deeper things of God may become more aware of temptations greater than ever before.

We shouldn't be surprised when temptation arises; in fact we need to discern when it is happening as well as honestly recognise that temptation can look and sound and feel extremely enticing as it seeks to deceive and entrap us (otherwise it wouldn't be tempting!). At that moment, we have decisions to make about which path we are going to choose: fleeting superficial pleasure or the freedom of a clear conscience and a further step towards maturity.

b) *Prior preparation; the slow and steady building of a godly life*

Look at the example of Joseph in Genesis 39. Verse 2 says that the Lord was with Joseph, and he was a successful man. Joseph took the trouble to maintain a close walk with God, before the time of testing arose, so that he would be in a better position to resist when the heat was on. That is what is required of us in day-to-day life (1 Thess. 5:16-18).

A number of sins can occur because we have already decided to engage in them earlier in the day. This is where a clear prior decision to avoid at all costs the particular areas of temptation needs to be made. This is of course not easy, and we very much need His help to do this. By His grace, we seek to build a more fulfilling life in Christ through a vital relationship with Him and others, a clear sense of vocation and continued growth in all areas of our being.

c) *Ruthless decision-making in the moment*

We are told to resist the devil (Js. 4:7) and flee temptation (Gen. 39:12; 2 Tim. 2:22). It is important to make this distinction as we shouldn't try and resist temptation if that means that we are trying harder and harder not to fall when we are still right in the midst of a tempting situation. If we have a vulnerability to excessive alcohol consumption, we shouldn't be entering an off licence in the first place.

When push comes to shove, inevitable temptation will bring us to a point of decision where we can choose righteousness by His enabling, or not. In that moment, it may feel as if it is impossible to proceed along the path of holiness, as if everything within us is crying out for satisfaction through fulfilment of fleshly desire. It takes courage, ruthlessness, aggression, a willingness to die to self in order to choose Christ when temptation is buffeting us. And yet this is what we are called to do, this is the stuff of practical Christianity, what it means to gradually become the person He is shaping us to be.

Exercising the power of choice early is crucial. As soon as we are in a situation of temptation, we need to realise that we have the ability to choose righteously, say 'no' and move away from the source of temptation. I have heard of one leader who determines to try and do that within five seconds; the longer the delay, the harder it becomes to pull away.

It has been the experience of many saints in Christ that the most challenging moment is just prior to making the decision to break free – once the decision is made, and not necessarily before, people have repeatedly testified that a fresh sense of empowering follows which reinforces the reality and value of living by faith.

4) <u>The Bible teaches us a way of daily renewal and growth</u>

Gradual growth in holiness occurs through the process of putting off the old man (the fleshly/sinful nature and its desires), being renewed in the spirit of our minds, and putting on the new man (the very nature of Christ's that can become ours through faith; Rom. 12:1-2; 1 Cor. 2:16; Eph. 4:22-24; Col. 3:8-10). This involves knowing the deep positional change that the Holy Spirit has wrought in our hearts, and choosing to surrender to the life of Christ in us in order to experience the steady shaping of character that that brings.

This can be described as a divine exchange; in humility and repentance we bring our broken selves just as we are and in grateful submission, receive His righteousness and new ability to be like Christ in the here and now.

5) Removing idols of the heart

From a Christian perspective, an idol is anything that becomes to us more important than God Himself. That thing may not in itself be bad (e.g. relationships, work, hobbies etc.) but there is a problem if they become our primary source of security and satisfaction. Our task is to identify and cast away that which has taken the place of God as our primary object of desire and worship, such that our hearts are fully captivated by the Lord.

Another way of saying this is to avoid looking for life-giving water from wells which are empty. Jer. 2:13; 14:3:

> *"For my people have committed two evils;*
> *They have forsaken Me, the fountain of living waters,*
> *And hewn themselves cisterns – broken cisterns that can hold no water.*
>
> *Their nobles have sent their lads for water;*
> *They went to the cisterns and found no water.*
> *They returned with their vessels empty;*
> *They were ashamed and confounded*
> *And covered their heads."*

6) <u>Learn to walk in the Spirit</u>

God has provided a means for us to live in such a way that we can be consistently controlled and directed by the Holy Spirit in every area of our lives, that we may not fulfil the lust of the flesh (Rom. 8:14; Gal. 5:16; Eph. 5:18). This means that we can be spiritually-minded, setting our minds on things above and not on the earth, and have a passionate desire to walk in His ways (Rom. 8:6; Col. 3:2). This then leads to the manifestation of the fruit of the Spirit (Gal. 5:22-23) which reflects the character of Christ and brings God glory. As we submit to the Spirit, He will lead us into all truth (Jn. 14:26; 16:13) and help us to abide in Him through the anointing within (1 Jn. 2:27).

7) <u>The importance of discipline, self-control and godly habits</u>

We have been given a spirit of power and of love and of a sound mind (2 Tim. 1:7). Therefore, we have the ability to live disciplined lives by the power of the Spirit, though of course this will at first not come easily, particularly if we have already been neglectful in this area for some time. The formation of spiritual discipline can lead to the breaking of bad, destructive behavioural cycles and to the establishment of positive, biblical behaviour that will produce God-glorifying results in due course. As the famous saying goes:

> 'Sow a thought, reap an action; sow an action, reap a habit; sow a habit, reap a character; sow a character, reap a destiny.'[6]

Divine cooperation

Especially in this area of growth towards godliness, it is important to remember that this is the outworking of the Spirit in our lives as we respond to His grace in repentance, faith, surrender and obedience. It is not simply a matter of trying harder. At the same time, disciplined effort is required, and a commitment to acting rightly even when we may not feel like it.

Phil. 2:12-13 strikes this balance:

> *Therefore, my beloved, as you have always obeyed, not as in my presence only, but now much more in my absence, work out your own salvation with fear and trembling; for it is God who works in you both to will and to do for His good pleasure.*

Jerry Bridges uses a helpful term to describe this synergism – 'dependent responsibility' – which captures the essence of God's grace cooperating with man's graft in order to produce Christ-centred growth. He writes of the Puritans:

> *The age of the English Puritans in the seventeenth century was undoubtedly the most influential era of English evangelicalism. Their books and sermons, even with their difficult-to-read prose, are still being reprinted, read, and profited from today in all the English-speaking nations. The Puritans understood the concept of dependent responsibility. They used to say (and this is not an exact quote but captures their attitude), "Work as if it all depends on you, yet pray as if it all depends on God."* [7]

Some people rightly criticise the pithy maxim: 'Let go and let God', or the variant of this: 'Do your best and let God do the rest' (which I do like better). The concern is that these sentiments may lead to an overly presumptuous faith which minimises the effort and application required on man's part.

I actually think there is some truth in these statements, as long as we are clear about what we mean by them. It shouldn't refer to an abdication of personal responsibility and diligence and is certainly not a licence to just do whatever we want and feel like. Rather, it is a way of summarising the key dynamic in our walk with Him – that we are to surrender to His leading and guidance each and every moment whilst making constant good decisions to follow His ways even when this is hard.

On the whole, I do believe that the Christian life can be

characterised by a joyous dependence on the Lord, where we are continually being empowered by Him and where we find true rest for our souls (Matt. 11:28-30). At the same time, somewhat paradoxically at first glance, the Bible talks about the need for us to be diligent to enter into His rest (Heb. 4:9-11). It does take real effort to repent and submit and obey in order that we may come to abide with Him in a deep way. From that position of security and strength in Christ, we can then fruitfully 'work from a place of rest'[8].

TRUTH:

We enter into real spiritual conflict

The reality of spiritual warfare

This is often a missing link in the understanding of, experiences in and approaches to our faith, such that we fail to recognise the very real impact that unseen forces have on individual lives and whole communities/nations.

This section will only make sense if we understand and accept the reality of personified good and evil. A biblical worldview of the unseen world is crucial in order to gain a more comprehensive understanding of our faith journey[9]. There is a cosmic battle being played out for and in the souls of men and women. The fallen ruler of this world seeks to bring as many people down with him as possible. Our lives are thus being lived within the backdrop of ongoing spiritual conflict.

'Spiritual warfare' is a term used to describe the inevitable conflict that a Christian finds himself in (and opposition that he finds himself facing) upon entering the kingdom of God. Once we become part of the kingdom of light, we automatically enter into real, often fervent, spiritual conflict with the kingdom of darkness (2 Cor. 10:3-6; Eph. 6:10-20; Js. 4:1-4 etc.). (As you can see, I interchange the terms 'spiritual conflict' and 'spiritual warfare', only to try and avoid some of the potential excesses, e.g. 'seeing demons behind every problem', that might be associated with some usages of the latter term.)

It is the testimony of many serious Christians that as they press in to know God in deeper ways, they become much more aware of the real spiritual battle that ensues within and without. Some mature leaders in the faith have reminded us that:

- The internal warfare between flesh and Spirit is the normal Christian life and
- The more we grow, the more sin we see (and the more intense the conflict seems to become at times)[10].

It has also been said that the followers of Christ can discern the greatest opposition in areas where the Lord might be doing His greatest work in a given situation. This can be a source of encouragement for us to persevere in the things He has called us to, even when it feels like we are hitting some significant barriers.

The enemies of our soul

To recap and continue on from chapter 3, a common Christian understanding is that we battle with (in various combinations at different times):

1) The devil and his cohorts, who seek to influence the hearts and minds of men and nations for his evil purposes.

2) The flesh which is the sinful nature within us, including unhealthy patterns of thought and behaviour programmed within our neural networks and manifested in some of our automatic responses particularly when we are under pressure. Although in Christ we have already died to the intrinsic power that this has over us, if we step out of faith and obedience we render ourselves

vulnerable to a reemergence of the flesh and subsequent increased pull towards sin.

3) The world i.e. the anti-Christian system that we live in, that would seek to distort and eliminate the truth of God's existence and Word in all spheres of life.

It should be stressed that spiritual warfare is not hypothetical, esoteric or occurring in a different reality from daily existence. It is fought on the battlefield of everyday, mundane life, from the time we have to get up in the mornings, to the way we take care of ourselves, relate to other people, conduct ourselves at work, use our free time, face crises as they arise etc.; we must be careful not to overspiritualise this topic because it is about the ordinary and expected Christian walk.

Fighting from a place of victory

It is important to keep very much in mind the crucial fact that the battle belongs to the Lord (1 Sam. 17:47) and He has already won the victory (Col. 2:15)! He fights on our behalf in ways that we sometimes cannot see or appreciate (2 Kgs. 6:6-18). He supplies us with the weapons of our warfare and the whole armour of God, which is Christ Himself (Rom. 13:14; 2 Cor. 10:3-6; Eph. 6:10-20).

We thus fight from a place of victory. Our task is to realise on this earth what has already been won in the spiritual realm:

D-Day and V-E Day

The significance for missions of Christ's victory over Satan on the cross has been illustrated by the Allies' success in invading Normandy on D-day in World War II. Once the Allies were successfully ashore and had established a secure beachhead, military experts on both sides knew that Germany's eventual defeat was assured. In fact, a failed attempt by some of Germany's military leaders to assassinate Hitler six weeks after D-day came partially because many in the German high command realised that the war would eventually be lost, and they hoped to install new leadership that could negotiate with the Western Allies. But though the victory in Normandy assured the Allies' eventual success, Germany still had a strong army. A full year of difficult fighting remained, and thousands of men, women and children would be killed or wounded before the war was over.

In the same way, the death and resurrection of Christ have secured a certain, final victory of Satan, but he is still a strong, vicious, determined enemy. His work to deceive and destroy the nations and harm believers continues to result in great damage. The war will not be over until Christ returns to utterly destroy Satan's work. In the meantime, the work of missions is at the front line of the ongoing battle, as Satan's rule is assaulted and defeated through the advance of the gospel.[11]

The way in which we engage in spiritual warfare is not mystical, excessive, dramatic etc. but it is faithful obedience to the will of God, empowered by His Spirit in big and small things. It is about living for His glory moment-by-moment. Consistent obedience (and to some degree 'ignoring' the enemy, whilst staying focused on the Lord) can be the best form of warfare.

APPLICATION:

The experience of spiritual conflict can strengthen our character

---

Knowing where the battle is

As put forward in chapter 3, understanding spiritual conflict/

warfare helps us to gain a clearer and more realistic view of the world as it is. Whilst still quite imperfectly, we are able to have a suitably nuanced understanding of why there is much pain and suffering in this world, and much conflict between the peoples and nations of it. We have an appreciation of an invisible dimension that can profoundly influence what we see and experience.

So, particularly in areas of interpersonal conflict, we are able to remind ourselves that we do not wrestle against flesh and blood (Eph. 6:12) and that the weapons of our warfare are not carnal but mighty in God (2 Cor. 10:4). Instead of becoming desperately frustrated with people and situations which seem at the time to be beyond meaningful change, we can wisely consider the contributory role of unseen forces.

This means that a lot of spiritual warfare will be conducted on our knees, before the throne of God, in focused prayer rather than just in the midst of the specific situation. It is this praying through and 'winning the battle in the heavenlies' that can make a real difference to the outcome of a particular struggle we are having.

Spiritual warfare can be character-building

I think God allows the enemies of our soul to persist not just because the time for final judgement has not yet come but because He uses these pressures and resistances to build greater character within us.

I have often wondered why God does not simply remove all vulnerability towards sin and indeed make us somewhat impervious to the lure of temptation. I am equally as often reminded that the very things we struggle with are the very things which can remind us of our dependence on Him and which cause us to continually seek after Him for grace to overcome. It would indeed be a travesty if we were to be somehow reprogrammed not to sense any weakness and struggle – and ended up living in our own strength, apart from the truth and power of God.

God is keen to train our hands for the kind of war that He has called us to fight, the war to advance His kingdom. Being trained through effective engagement in spiritual warfare builds an essential warfare spirit deep within us that can help us to stand firm in challenging times, and be of real use to a lost world.

The following illustration, one of my favourites, shows the value of perseverance in the face of sometimes inexplicable resistance:

The unmoved rock

Once upon a time, there was a man who was sleeping at night in his cabin when suddenly his room filled with light and the Saviour appeared. The Lord told the man He had work for him to do, and showed him a large rock in front of his cabin. The Lord explained that the man was to push against the rock with all his might. This the man did, day after day. For many years he toiled from sun up to sun down, his shoulders set squarely against the cold, massive surface of the unmoving rock, pushing with all his might.

Each night the man returned to his cabin sore and worn out, feeling that his whole day had been spent in vain. Seeing that the man was showing signs of discouragement, Satan decided to enter the picture placing thoughts into the man's mind such as: "You have been pushing against that rock for a long time, and it hasn't budged. Why kill yourself over this? You are never going to move it." Thus giving the man the impression that the task was impossible and that he was a failure.

These thoughts discouraged and disheartened the man even more. "Why kill myself over this?" he thought. "I'll just put in my time, giving just the minimum of effort and that will be good enough." And that he planned to do until one day he decided to make it a matter of prayer and take his troubled thoughts to the Lord.

"Lord," he said, "I have laboured long and hard in your service, putting all my strength to do what you have asked –

Yet, after all this time, I have not even budged that rock a half a millimetre. What is wrong? Why am I failing?" To this the Lord responded compassionately, "My child, when long ago I asked you to serve me and you accepted, I told you that your task was to push against the rock with all your strength, which you have done. Never once did I mention to you that I expected you to move it. Your task was to push.

And now you come to me, your strength spent, thinking that you have failed. But, is that really so? Look at yourself. Your arms are strong and muscled, your back sinewed and brown, your hands are callused from constant pressure, and your legs have become massive and hard. Through opposition, you have grown much and your abilities now surpass that which you used to have. Yet you haven't moved the rock. But your calling was to be obedient and to push and to exercise your faith and trust in My wisdom. This you have done. I, my child, will now move the rock." [12]

Towards maturity

How does this relate to mental health/wellbeing?

This is all part of God's plan to help His people grow in maturity, which is a core component of the definition on mental health that is used in this book. Learning well in and through spiritual warfare develops Christlike character which renders us increasingly useful for the work of the kingdom.

There is a grace (marked by noticeable wisdom and strength) that comes only from 'the school of hard knocks', from walking and fighting through many battles, from not always winning but always enduring/persevering in faith. The benefits and rewards of this may not be seen physically or materially but what price can be put on a spirit that has been trained in godliness and is mature enough to face any situation (1 Tim. 4:7-8; Js. 1:2-4)?

Chapter 6

ETERNAL PERSPECTIVE

The gospel is a divine story that spans all eternity.

It begins in the mind of God Himself and culminates in the fulfilment of His glorious purposes. Time and history as we know it is but one defined phase within the eternal narrative of God's grace.

In this chapter, we reflect upon how holding an eternal perspective on life can have a positive impact on our mental health. This is in itself of course a radical view because the very existence of such a thing as life after death is nowhere near being a settled fact in the scientific world. This is yet another example of how different a Christian worldview can be compared to prevailing norms, though by no means in a bad way necessarily.

Consider the following truths of the gospel and their potential applications to the area of mental health:

TRUTH:

This world is passing away, and a better reality is to come

The reality of Christian eschatology (or 'the study of last things')

Christians believe that the universe had a defined beginning, and that all that was brought into existence is headed towards a final purpose which has been ordained by God Himself.

If we are honest about it, within a secular, naturalistic society, this can sound like a most bizarre belief, and one for which the kind of evidence that would satisfy a sceptical scientist cannot be produced. Indeed, the statements and claims of Jesus Christ Himself were highly controversial at the time, forcing people to make up their minds as to whether, as C. S. Lewis summarised it, He was a liar, lunatic or Lord.

And yet, believers firmly hold on to views about the reality of things to come; this is because eschatology is but one part of a whole systematic theology derived from the Word of God, and that our faith is in the veracity of the message in its totality. We are convinced that the Bible is inspired by the Spirit of truth, that numerous Old Testament prophecies have been historically fulfilled, that such a person as Jesus Christ walked upon this earth to signal the arrival of the new kingdom of God. We believe in the depth of our beings that He died for the sins of the world, was raised to life on the third day, and that He is one day coming again.

The nature of Christian eschatology

The area of Christian eschatology can be a theological minefield. There are many different views surrounding the details of key prophetic events as described in the Bible including:

- The return of Jesus Christ
- A millennial rule with an associated rapture of believers and period of tribulation
- The end of the world and final judgement

- The world to come where His created beings will exist in their eternal state[1]

There would be many differing views as to the exact nature of these events. Beware of those who are too certain of their predictions. The best minds can see things very differently and we have to accept that our overall understanding is limited.

Unity (in diversity) in eschatology

Nevertheless, unity about essentials can be found in the midst of diverse opinions about secondary matters:

What is clear is that for followers of Christ, there is much to look forward to beyond this current existence. The Bible gives a vision of redeemed humanity living in eternal communion with its loving God through the saving work of the one true Mediator (Jn. 3:16; 1 Tim. 2:5). We will be granted resurrection bodies that will not know sickness or death (1 Cor. 15:42-44; Phil. 3:21).

There will be rewards for faithful service (1 Cor. 3:12-14; 2 Cor. 5:10). Evil will be finally judged and done away with (Rev. 20). The church will be presented as the bride of Christ that has been prepared for Him throughout the ages (Rev. 21:2). God will wipe away every tear from our eyes (Rev. 21:4). And then that great and awesome privilege: we will see Him for who He is (1 Cor. 13:12; 1 Jn. 3:2; Rev. 22:4). We will have the joy of dwelling with Him forever in the new heavens and new earth (Is. 65:17; 2 Pet. 3:13; Rev. 21:1).

The fact is that things are moving in the way God wants (although the sobering thought is that the Bible describes things getting worse before they improve). God is steadily progressing the path of creation towards a time when all things will find their consummation in Christ and the heavens truly declare His glory. A better, deeper, majestic reality is on the horizon.

APPLICATION:

We can have a pilgrim mentality whilst on this earth

Our temporary passage

1 Jn. 2:15-17:

> *Do not love this world or the things in the world. If anyone loves the world, the love of the Father is not in him. For all that is in the world – the lust of the flesh, the lust of the eyes, and the pride of life – is not of the Father but is of the world. And the world is passing away, and the lust of it; but he who does the will of God abides forever.*

The Word of God speaks of our earthly lives as a passing vapour that appears for a little time and then vanishes away (Js. 4:14). We are referred to as sojourners and pilgrims, who are to abstain from fleshly lusts which war against the soul (1 Pet. 2:11). This doesn't mean that we should devalue our lives or become disinterested and careless about how we conduct ourselves in this life. It does mean that we are to move ahead with a clear understanding that our time on this earth is relatively short, that our present being is for a specific purpose of God and that our real home lies in a place beyond what we now see.

Jesus spoke vividly about the dangers of becoming too attached to life in this world. He exhorts His followers to 'hate' their lives in this world (when viewed in comparison to the life to come), knowing that the blessed consequence of doing so will be reaped in eternity (Jn. 12:25). He urges us to consider what it would profit a man to gain the whole world but lose his own soul (Matt. 16:26;

Mk. 8:36). The apostle Paul lived with a constant readiness to be with Christ in the other world, unless the Lord preserved Him for a life of service to others in this one (Phil. 1:21-24).

Not too attached to this world

With this in mind, we can avoid a couple of pitfalls that can have an adverse influence on our whole beings, including our mental health:

1) We do not have to become overly invested in this world in a physical/material sense

We live in societies that can place excessive value on external success as represented by money, power, fame etc. In such settings, it is easy to succumb to the pressure of trying to accumulate more and more by way of personal possessions, influence and status, or to the despair whenever we realise that such things (to the degree that we desire them) are beyond our resources to attain.

By all means, as faithful stewards of the gifts of God, we should seek to live with a spirit of excellence and be as 'successful' as His grace enables us to be, for the benefit of His kingdom. However, we want to be able to be free from the driving force of unhealthy ambition and live with the kind of deep contentment that firmly defies the god of materialism.

Jesus said in Matt. 6:19-20:

> *"Do not lay up for yourselves treasures on earth, where moth and rust destroy and where thieves break in and steal; but lay up for yourselves treasures in heaven, where neither moth nor rust destroys and where thieves do not break in and steal."*

2) We do not have to become overly invested in a psychological/emotional sense

What I mean by this is that we do not have to expect to find true and lasting happiness in this world itself. Whilst, by the grace of God, we may experience much gladness through positive life events, the fulfilment of goals and ambitions, satisfying relationships etc., we do not have to place all our hopes on this world to bring us the kind of abiding joy that God desires for us. We can be freed from the pursuit of happiness as the main goal of this life, seeking a godly contentment which is great gain (1 Tim. 6:6-7).

In spite of the passing pleasures that this world can supply, are you deeper down in your soul weary of the imperfection and incompleteness, and hardship and struggle (even apparently trivial ones), so evident this side of eternity[2]? Do you yearn for a better time ahead, when the visible and invisible hindrances to a holy life will fall away in the light of His glory? Are you keenly aware of the tension between the now and the not yet in terms of the realisation of God's kingdom? Do you regularly conclude, "There must be more to life than this..."?

Well, I would say that that is a normal, even healthy, Christian experience, a sign that our hearts have their destiny in things above and beyond, a recognition that even the best that this world has to offer cannot remotely compare to what God has in store.

Open-handed living

I once heard of a university professor who would announce to his class at the start of a term that he had already given all of them an 'A' grade for the year. Now, I would of course question the ethics of this but I like his idea. The assurance of a good final outcome allowed his students to both relax and excel, concentrating fully on giving their best without the fearful pressure of not knowing what would become of them.

Whenever we gain an eternal perspective on our lives, it frees us to live with a confident, light-hearted abandonment to the sovereign will of God, knowing that we can faithfully pour ourselves out during our lives on this earth, but that our real home is in heaven where we will be with our beautiful Saviour and Lord forever.

The stress of having to accumulate and achieve and the anxious need to be happy now can both fade away as we develop a properly engaged but healthily unattached attitude to this world. This can bring about a peace of mind that is priceless. We do not have to spend unnecessary time and energy protecting reputations, striving to impress others, searching for any kind of significance. We can indeed live 'light and free', with much less invested concern for the temporal things that this world would call precious.

We can also rest in the knowledge that our own personal growth and transformation need not be forced or hurried. I am certain that in many ways I will not have been perfected by the time I leave this existence. I am thrilled to know that He has all eternity to work on me, and that He is not rushing to conform me into the image of His Son before my earthly days come to an end.

TRUTH:

God brings strength, meaning and hope in the midst of trials and tribulations

---

The reality of pain and suffering

Pain and suffering is everywhere in this fallen world.

We see this on a global scale with wars, famine, natural disasters etc. afflicting masses of humanity. We watch tragedy strike on a personal level; human beings suffer premature bereavement, chronic painful illness, financial disaster etc. which can shake them and their worlds to the core. We experience it on a daily, practical level; people struggle with regret about choosing the wrong career or spouse, battle with anxiety about whether they are competent enough to do what they do, wrestle with guilt over a bad habit that won't go away etc.

Christians are of course not immune to any of this. Indeed, we are called to suffer with and for Christ (Rom. 8:17-18; 2 Cor. 4:16-17; Phil. 1:29); in some parts of the world, believers are being actively persecuted for their faith, even to the point of martyrdom.

How we face suffering is a sure measure of how far we have progressed on the journey of maturity. I have often wondered whether the call to suffer more is for believers who are already steadily maturing i.e. almost as if He needs to grow and prepare us with increasingly difficult challenges before He can test us further with harder suffering (in order to purify us further), as if those who do not appear to have a more intimate knowledge of significant suffering are perhaps not ready enough to go through it!

The Bible presents a robust view of suffering

In the absence of a godly framework of understanding, we settle for evolutionary explanations of human evil and selfishness, and the sometimes cruel randomness of a guideless universe. This is enough for some, and the pain and suffering is put up with and shrugged off as part and parcel of natural existence that operates with a governing principle of luck. For others, the realities of a truly broken world could precipitate an existential crisis for which real and hopeful answers are required to calm a confused and questioning mind.

In Christ, we have the essentials (but not all the details) of a cogent explanation of the existence of turmoil and trouble in this world[3]. Earlier chapters have touched on the multifaceted causes of ongoing spiritual conflict, pervasive sin, debilitating sickness and 'unexplained' suffering. We gain blessed assurance that in the age to come, each of these precursors of pain will be put away once and for all.

The book of Job is a key place to go if we are looking for a more profound comprehension of suffering[4]. Here was a highly righteous man who suffered greatly for no obvious reason. But it was the not so obvious reasons for his suffering that have been preserved as crucial lessons for all of humanity throughout the ages.

We are given insight into how God tests people for His glory, the reality of external evil influences and the great sovereignty of an Almighty God. What is remarkable is that Job persevered in faith even though he didn't have the book of Job to read in order to understand the bigger back story!

In Christ, there is strength, meaning and hope for those who suffer

The fact of the matter is that for the time being, we often cannot grasp the meaning of our suffering, or find the answers that can lift us out of its depths. We are left simply with the task of hanging in there, trying to stay afloat, whilst starkly honest questions reverberate in our heads and unresolved angst afflicts our emotions.

God does not need us to pretend that everything is fine with our lives. He knows our struggles and wants us to bring our pain and frustration to Him, openly expressing what we are thinking and how we are feeling; He can well cope with our confusion and complaints. We must not think that we cannot be real when we come into His holy presence.

In the midst of suffering, gaining an eternal perspective on trials and tribulations, with an appreciation of the underpinning promises and purposes of God, can help us find His strength and discover the meaning and hope that He intends for us to have.

APPLICATION:

We can experience the grace to endure difficulty

He supplies grace in adversity

The Bible has a lot to say about trials and how to view them from a godly perspective. They are presented to us as part and parcel of the normal Christian life, instruments that God uses to work out His will in and for our lives (Rom. 5:3-5; 2 Cor. 4:16-18; Heb. 12:5-11; Js. 1:2-4, 12; 1 Pet. 1:6-9; 4:12-19).

One of the most challenging exhortations in the Word of God is to rejoice in all situations, including having joy in the midst of trials (Phil. 4:4; 1 Thess. 5:16-18; Js. 1:2-4). This seems so counterintuitive and exceptionally difficult – it is! It only begins to become possible when we have a good theological understanding of the place of suffering in the Christian life and His sustaining and overcoming grace, when we grasp the vision of an infinitely good God who is deeply interested in the shaping of our lives and moulding of our character.

He comforts us in our tribulation, that our experience of His grace in time of need will help us to support others. 2 Cor. 1:3-5:

> *Blessed be the God and Father of our Lord Jesus Christ, the Father of mercies and God of all comfort, who comforts us in all our tribulation, that we may be able to comfort those who are in any trouble, with the comfort with which we ourselves are comforted by God. For as the sufferings of Christ abound in us, so our consolation also abounds through Christ.*

Components of grace for trials

Whilst we suffer, in Christ there can be found:

1) Strength

When there seems to be no immediate solution to our dilemmas, He can provide the grace to endure within and persevere through them. We like the first parts of 1 Cor. 10:13 that talk about God not allowing us to be tempted beyond what we are able, and that He makes the way of escape. But the verse ends with '...that you may be able to bear it'. He doesn't necessarily take us out of our pressing situation but helps us to go through it in order that we will come out the other side stronger in Him.

Js. 1:2-4 has helped carry me through many a difficult time:

> *My brethren, count it all joy when you fall into various trials, knowing that the testing of your faith produces patience. But let patience have its perfect work, that you may be perfect and complete, lacking nothing.*

Endurance and perseverance are goals in themselves (see also Heb. 12:1; Js. 1:12). Sometimes all we are enabled to do is to keep on keeping on in spite of how difficult things are. This is not a passive, pessimistic clinging on for dear life but rather a settled confidence that whatever we are facing, He will eventually bring us through such that we become even more fit for His eternal purposes. When our faith is tested, our endurance has a chance to grow and when it is fully developed, maturity of character ensues. We know that He will finish that good work which He has started in us (Phil. 1:6).

One of the most encouraging sermons I've listened to, just when I needed to hear it, was delivered by pastor Stephen Gaukroger. It was during a time when our youngest child, for various reasons, was reaching nearly five years of not being able to sleep through the night, with resultant exhaustion for both parents. Feeling quite discouraged and at our wits' end after having attempted all known strategies to try and rectify the situation, a phrase leapt out of his message on faithful perseverance and struck with me with Spirit-inspired clarity and relevance: "...this too shall pass". Those four small words brought much comfort and hope at the time and that phase of life, long since passed and perhaps trivial in comparison with other scenarios of suffering, has become but an instructive memory as well as an encouragement to others who struggle.

2) <u>Meaning</u>

Heb. 12:5-6:

> *And you have forgotten the exhortation which speaks to you*
> *as to sons:*
> *"My son, do not despise the chastening of the Lord,*
> *Nor be discouraged when you are rebuked by Him;*
> *For whom the Lord loves He chastens,*
> *And scourges every son whom He receives."*

It is hardly the case that we will always understand why we are going through a particular challenge or trial. Often the reasons are hidden from us (remember Job) and we are left with the decision of whether to lose heart or trust in the One who has promised to be our refuge and strength, a very present help in trouble (Ps. 46:1). In times like these we are going to be so dependent on His wisdom and discernment to be able to see His hand at work even when things feel as if they are falling apart.

We do know that for those who earnestly seek after Him, He is doing an ever deeper work in their lives. As we go through the struggle of suffering and are forced to deal with the key issues at hand, we can have the grace to turn to Him and learn His ways in the midst of them, with the end result of a further maturing of our character. Sometimes He needs to prepare us on the inside before we are ready to take the next step in our journey of faith. A newly formed butterfly needs to struggle within its cocoon before being able to break out with wings strong enough to fly.

How do we cope with seemingly senseless injustice and suffering? What about innocent civilians being killed in bomb strikes, babies born with severe physical malformations, the loss of a loved one before their time? There are no easy answers. For a long time we may not even find any adequate answers. But what we do have is the opportunity to honestly bring our crisis and pain to the One who knows all things, asking that He reveal to us His deeper and mysterious ways and praying that we can grasp the sense of all things working for His ultimate glory.

3) <u>Hope</u>

When we are suffering, it is not wrong to yearn for a time when we will be truly free, when God will wipe away every tear from our eyes and there will be no more death, nor sorrow nor pain (Rev. 21:4). It is this hope that enables us to find more strength and meaning in our trials.

He will eventually make all things right; our trust is in a loving and just God who will one day make sense of that which now seems incomprehensible. Our hardest questions will be addressed or become irrelevant in the glory of eternity; justice will be done and wounds will eventually be healed. We surely know that all things work together for good to those who love God and are called according to His purpose (Rom. 8:28).

What also give us hope are the lasting benefits that come from having gone through major difficulties by the grace of God. As described above, we develop sympathy, empathy and compassion for others (2 Cor. 1:3-5). It produces a depth of character and maturity that cannot be gained elsewhere (Js. 1:2-4). And there is a promise of great reward for those who endure. Js. 1:12:

> *Blessed is the man who endures temptation; for when he has been approved, he will receive the crown of life which the Lord has promised to those who love Him.*

So, whenever we can embrace a God-centred approach (fuelled by an eternal perspective) to the very real trials of life that will surely come our way, we equip ourselves to potentially be able to face all situations with strength, meaning and hope. This can have a positive impact on our mental health particularly in terms of reducing apprehension and fear (and hence some forms of anxiety) and discouragement and despair (and hence some forms of depression).

Refiner's fire

I came across this story which highlights the work of God in testing and refining us such that we will reflect His image with greater brightness (Ps. 66:10):

> I received the following illustration from a friend and refer to it often when I am in the midst of the fire. I want to share it with you:
>
> Malachi 3:3 says:
>
> "He will sit as a refiner and purifier of silver."
>
> This verse puzzled some women in a Bible study and they wondered what this statement meant about the character and nature of God. One of the women offered to find out the process of refining silver and get back to the group at their next Bible Study.
>
> That week, the woman called a silversmith and made an appointment to watch him at work. She didn't mention anything about the reason for her interest beyond her curiosity about the process of refining silver.
>
> As she watched the silversmith, he held a piece of silver over the fire and let it heat up. He explained that in refining silver, one needed to hold the silver in the middle of the fire where the flames were hottest as to burn away all the impurities.

The woman thought about God holding us in such a hot spot; then she thought again about the verse that says: "He sits as a refiner and purifier of silver."

She asked the silversmith if it was true that he had to sit there in front of the fire the whole time the silver was being refined. The man answered that yes, he not only had to sit there holding the silver, but he had to keep his eyes on the silver the entire time it was in the fire. If the silver was left a moment too long in the flames, it would be destroyed.

The woman was silent for a moment. Then she asked the silversmith, "How do you know when the silver is fully refined?" He smiled at her and answered, "Oh, that's easy — when I see my image in it."[5]

TRUTH:

We are destined to rule and reign with Him

A glorious future awaits

2 Tim. 2:10-12a:

> *Therefore I endure all things for the sake of the elect, that they also may obtain the salvation which is in Christ Jesus with eternal glory.*
> *This is a faithful saying:*
> *For if we died with Him, we shall also live with Him.*
> *If we endure, we shall also reign with Him.*

Right from the first book of the Bible, we see that God's purpose for man includes him subduing and having dominion over the earth (Gen. 1:26-28). He has put something in us that calls us to have authority and leadership over that which He has placed under us so that we will reflect God's rule of justice and mercy.

Jesus taught parables that show how managing well what God has given in this life is a prerequisite for ruling over many things in the future; our faithfulness now determines our usefulness then (e.g. Matt. 24:45-47). I can think of no better thing to hear at the end of our earthly journey than the words of Christ in Matt. 25: 21, 23:

> *"His lord said to them, 'Well done, good and faithful servant; you were faithful over a few things, I will make you ruler over many things. Enter into the joy of your lord.'"*

Paul the apostle tells us that as sin reigned in death, even so grace might reign through righteousness to eternal life through Jesus Christ our Lord (Rom. 5:21). He talks about a time when the saints will judge the world, and angels (1 Cor. 6:2-3).

God has raised us up together and made us sit together in the heavenly places in Christ Jesus (Eph. 2:6). Rev. 20:4 mentions resurrected saints who reign with Christ for a thousand years.

Specific work to be done

The Bible doesn't allow us to hold on to a caricature of heaven as portrayed in popular culture. Life in the eternal state will not be ethereal, vague or without form. Physical creation will continue in the form of a 'new earth' (2 Pet. 3:31; Rev. 21:1); creation itself will be delivered from the bondage of corruption into the glorious liberty of the children of God (Rom. 8:21). We will be functioning within real, resurrected bodies (1 Cor. 15:42-55; Phil. 3:21).

And eternity is not going to be boring. Think not of winged beings floating around playing harps, or a massive choir singing never ending choruses. Worship will of course be the atmosphere of heaven but not in the sense of an everlasting Sunday morning service.

1 Cor. 2:9 (quoting Is. 64:4; 65:17):

> *"Eye has not seen, nor ear heard,*
> *Nor have entered into the heart of man*
> *The things which God has prepared for those who love*
> *Him."*

There will be specific work for us to do as part of ruling and reigning with Him in the new heavens and new earth. In His unfathomable wisdom, He has chosen to involve man in His ultimate dominion over all things.

God's design is for the world to be run by human beings, in cooperation with Him (a meaning contained in the phrase 'made in the image of God'); as N. T. Wright says: 'God wants humans to be wisely in charge of things'.

Preparation for what is ahead

So, believers in Christ are people of two homes, a temporary one on earth and a permanent one in heaven. We are on mission whilst in this life, with our eyes firmly fixed on what is going to be lasting. This gives us two key tasks to devote our lives to in the here and now:

Firstly, we want to be used by God to help bring as many people into the knowledge of Him as possible through the words of our testimony and witness of our character. We want to have the same goal as Jesus who came to seek and save that which was lost (Lk. 19:10).

Secondly, we want to allow God to mould us and shape us in any way He desires that we may be well prepared for a life in eternity where we will serve and lead in His kingdom for His glory. Attitude, character and skills are all being developed as we walk through the stages and seasons of life, towards our destiny of being and working with Him forever.

APPLICATION:

Our lives now are a preparation for future work in His kingdom

What we do now really matters

The question of what we are going to do with our lives is a very important one. Finding our place in this world in terms of work and vocation is a crucial task, such that we can maximise the opportunities to express what we are good at and what we enjoy doing, for the benefit of others. Discovering one's 'vision' in life is a common way of describing this activity.

And yet we need grace in this area too. The dreams that we carry in our hearts are not always fulfilled, at least not in the timescale that we would desire. The disappointment of unfulfilled expectations can be a heavy thing to hold. Some people are living too much in and for the future in the sense that they cannot allow themselves to be content unless some imagined goal has been achieved. This can leave them in a 'neither here nor there' state: not fully engaged in what they are called to now, and yet to reach where they think they are eventually being led to be.

For those who are seeking to do His will at all times, an understanding that God is very much at work now, where we are, even if the circumstances are challenging, is an antidote to unsettled restlessness and the temptation to move away both mentally and in practice to a place that we are not yet ready for.

If our daily decisions are being subjected to His wisdom and guidance, there can be an assurance that He is sovereignly working out His plans and purposes, and is using life in the moment to accomplish precious inner transformation as He takes us on towards the fulfilment of our vision and calling. He does this whilst we are in the middle of our personal lives, our family commitments, our time in the workplace etc.; every challenge and difficulty we face can become an opportunity to grow in the kind of faith and obedience that will have value for all eternity.

Fully alive in all situations

Thus, with a perspective of what God is doing in light of all eternity, each part of each day can become infused with the kind of meaning and purpose that inspires life and ushers in grace whenever the going gets tough.

When I think of how God's salvation message has applications to the down-to-earth practicalities of everyday life, an idea that comes to mind is that we can experience a 'gospel of the mundane'. By this I mean that the truth and power of the gospel can come bearing down in the seemingly insignificant affairs of daily existence, such that they become moments of grace and offerings of worship. In all situations, we can open up our hearts to God in surrendered prayer, asking that His very presence will fill the place where we are.

Getting out of bed on a cold winter's morning can be done with gratitude for each cool breath that can be had and another opportunity to bring the warmth of God's love to those we will be interacting with. Like Brother Lawrence in *Practising the presence of God*, washing pots and pans can become a cheerful activity of God-glorifying service. Periods of conflict with a loved one, submitted to the Lord with openness to His Word, can give rise to new areas of learning and a deepening of relationship such that the grace of God becomes even more real to whom we are interacting with.

I like what I once saw on a notice:

> *Happy moments, praise God.*
> *Difficult moments, seek God.*

Quiet moments, worship God.
Painful moments, trust God.
Every moment, thank God.

Christianity is for ordinary people, who go on to live quietly extraordinary lives by the Spirit of God. We must not get distracted by Christian 'celebrities' or 'superstars' whose large and prominent ministries seem to ooze spiritual success. The normal Christian walk is not flashy or high-profile. I would say that most of the greatest heavenly rewards will be given to those who have lived faithful lives regardless of their circumstances, most of whom the watching world will have known nothing about.

The worthy goal of maturity

A constant theme throughout this book has been maturity, both as a key aspect of our definition of mental health/wellbeing as well as the goal of His sanctifying work in our lives through the Holy Spirit.

I like the definition of maturity (that comes as a result of counting it all joy and persevering in trials) in Js. 1:4 i.e. 'lacking nothing'. To me, this does not mean that we reach a stage in this life where we have finally 'arrived' – Phil. 3:12-14 describes the continual nature of our pursuit of God's call – but that we have learnt how to be secure in our relationship with God, where our basic needs are being met in Christ and we are free to flourish in the present moment.

When we realise that He is actively shaping and preparing us for what lies ahead, we can better face our challenges and difficulties knowing that character is steadily being built. In fact, our attitude should be one of not wanting to move onto other things until we have learnt the lessons that He has for us where we are.

I came to faith as a late-teen and soon joined the Christian Fellowship at the A-Level College I enrolled in. It was a happy time together, getting to know the Lord better in the context of fun and loving fellowship. And yet from that early stage, I was aware, along with others, that the Christian walk was going to involve strain, struggle and stretching as the Holy Spirit went about His purifying work. There was a particular prayer that arose each time we gathered to meet with God:

"Lord, don't let us miss any lessons that You may be wanting to teach us right now. We are willing to really learn them. If necessary, don't let us move on to the next stage until we have passed the tests that you have set before us at this moment in time."

Chapter 7

OUR RESPONSE

The gospel of God invites a response from man.

The truths of the gospel are made plain and convincing by the power and revelation of the Holy Spirit but this does not mean that people are automatically converted and become disciples of Christ – otherwise the whole world would be believing.

The Holy Spirit is at work in individuals, drawing them closer and bringing them to a point of decision as regards what to do with the claims of Christ.

What is remarkable is, in His grace:

- He helps us to make an appropriate response
- Even the responses themselves can bring us joy and freedom when made with the right attitude of heart.

Consider the following responses which enable the gospel to become real and vital in our lives:

Core responses: the 'always attitudes

What they are

There are several responses that we are continually making as Christian disciples; I call them the 'always attitudes'. God Himself helps us to respond in this way; He enabled us to make the initial response and empowers us to make an ongoing response to what He has done and provided.

Consider the following:

1) <u>Repentance</u>

This is the gift God has given to us in Christ to enable sin to be truly acknowledged, confessed and dealt with so that we can continue on in a relationship of peace with God whilst experiencing the peace of God.

This continual process of conviction, confession, and cleansing is like the 'backbone' of a redeemed sinner's walk with a holy God and enables us to live in grace moment-by-moment. Whilst conviction is holy and serious, repentance is meant to be an utterly freeing attitude and not one that brings discouragement and condemnation.

2) <u>Faith</u>

This is the appropriate response to revelation which is true. Christian faith is founded on fact, on the truth of God's Word, and not on blind opinion or subjective conclusions. It is believing (in) God; what He has said in His Word and what He promises to do.

It involves receiving grace freely and all that we can never do for ourselves, and acting accordingly as an outworking of faith. It is acting as if God's Word is true. Faith is the connection between what God has done for us (which we could never do for ourselves) and the experience of that truth and freedom in everyday life.

3) <u>Surrender</u>

This is an attitude which lays ourselves at the foot of the cross, ready to receive grace and be led into faithful obedience. It is acknowledging the grace of God, our broken and contrite heart, and the utter need of His help. It involves true humility, submission, abandonment, yielding, commitment, a tender heart, reliance and complete dependence on Him.

Our rights and reputation are no longer held onto but are given up to His Lordship. This 'stance' before the Lord is what helps to keep the flow of grace coming into our lives and subsequently pouring out in loving service to others.

4) <u>Obedience</u>

Obedience flows out of a broken, repentant heart that has received the grace of God through faith and is totally surrendered to His will. It is the natural outflow of a gospel-centred life. It involves 'doing the next right thing' to the best of our ability as we are strengthened by the Lord. It is a sign of our love for Him (Jn. 14:15; 15:10; 1 Jn. 5:2-3).

It includes making hard decisions that cost something in terms of time, energy and resources. It is the production of good works by His grace to complement and express our faith (Js. 2:17).

There is a place for discipline and diligence in doing the will of God, taking up the cross and laying aside our own selfish desires. There is also sometimes a need to act first, regardless of how we feel, trusting that positive feelings can follow once we have done the right thing in God's sight. Above all, obedience stems from the grace of God within our lives, and is enabled by it.

These responses are of course not isolated categories but are related to each other, and provide mutual facilitation of their simultaneous practice.

Why they are necessary

Whilst God remains sovereign, He has also ordained that man needs to exercise personal responsibility and choice in order to truly realise and express his loving faith towards God. He does not control us like robots but wants us to freely respond to the revelation of His grace.

The right response enables us to enter into a conscious, saving relationship with God for the first time and become secure in Him. This is what people describe as being converted or 'coming to faith in Christ'.

Continued right responses help us to live in the fullness of the Spirit moment-by-moment and grow towards maturity in Christ. They make it possible for us to be continually exposed to the wisdom and strength of God, which He delights to give.

Altogether, all the time, by His power

These core responses occur all together. Believers may sometimes ask which comes first – repentance or faith? Some would say repentance is required before true faith is born. Others would say the gift of faith is required before genuine repentance can occur. In my view, these two responses operate together, both being inspired by the Spirit of God.

The 'always attitudes' are so named because they constantly come into play when we are interacting with the Lord. As we walk with God throughout a typical day, our hearts are responding in repentance, faith, surrender and obedience all the time; it is this dynamic process that helps us to consistently walk in the Spirit.

It cannot be stressed enough how dependent we are on the grace of God to enable us to respond well to Him. As I have repeatedly said throughout this book, we can of ourselves do nothing, and that includes manufacturing a right heart response apart from the

Spirit's deep work within us.

Cultivating a close walk with the Lord

He helps us with this

Our relationship with God is not to be theoretical, intellectual or merely governed by a list of do's and don'ts. Whilst structure and discipline are important, walking with the Lord is meant to be a vibrant, energising, fruitful experience.

It is indeed a relationship where there is two-way communication, the security of acceptance and the clarity of our mission in this world.

God Himself enables us to maintain a close walk with Him through the cultivation of a deep and effective devotional life on a day-by-day, moment-by-moment basis. He grants us (among other things):

- The desire to spend time with Him
- The leading as to how to be and what to do in His presence
- The reality of spiritual connection leading on to daily empowering

Whilst there are general principles to consider, in cultivating a healthy devotional life, He does allow for individualisation of our approach to Him to fit in with our stage of growth, temperament, lifestyle, current season of life, other commitments etc.

There is no one right way of spending time with God, and there is a process of discovery involved in learning what works best for us as we seek to be close to Him.

Rhythms of communion with God

The essence of the devotional relationship with God is spending quality time with Him. Being with Jesus is a primary call of the Christian (Acts 4:13; 6:4). It is in this context that a deep abiding can be forged and transformation of the heart and mind can truly be achieved.

When we come into His presence with open and listening spirits, we make ourselves available to receive wisdom and strength from above for the very things we need to do each day. We get to experience His empowering in the midst of our weakness.

Dallas Willard gave this advice to a young John Ortberg who was seeking to be more effective in his ministry to others:

> *"You must arrange your days so that you are experiencing deep contentment, joy, and confidence in your everyday life with God.'*[1]

This communion with Him can happen at different times and in different ways:

1) Specific times

Ps. 27:4:

> *One thing I have desired of the Lord,*
> *That will I seek:*
> *That I may dwell in the house of the Lord*
> *All the days of my life,*
> *To behold the beauty of the Lord,*
> *And to enquire in His temple.*

Alongside a continual relationship with Him, we need to regularly draw aside for more concentrated periods of being with the Lord and seeking His face. Some people practice and recommend a daily set period at a particular time of day which is indeed commendable although can potentially lead to a pitfall if the believer's faith is placed more in the routine than God Himself who should be the object of worship.

Others might have a more flexible and fluid approach in which there is a balance between the continual walk with God and specific times spent in His presence, dictated by the needs and demands of the particular period of life. It is interesting to note that Jesus Himself would sometimes draw near to His father early at the start of the day (Mk. 1:35), at other times at the end of a period of ministry (Matt. 14:23), sometimes all throughout the night (Lk. 6:12).

What is important is that when we come to Him, we are able to be fully present in His presence, allowing ourselves sufficient time to quieten our spirits so that we can connect with who He is and what He is saying. The mature believer will have learnt how to 'pray through' and to stay in His presence until a quickening of the spirit and renewal of thoughts occurs.

The attitude that He is looking for is that we know how to prioritise the sitting at His feet to hear His word, that we are able to put aside the distracting hustle and bustle of daily life to spend the precious moments with Him that will enable us to face the world with His grace. Lk. 10:38-42 is very instructive:

> *Now it happened as they went that He entered a certain village; and a certain woman named Martha welcomed Him into her house. And she had a sister called Mary, who also sat at Jesus' feet and heard His word. But Martha was distracted with much serving, and she approached Him and said, "Lord, do You not care that my sister has left me to serve alone? Therefore tell her to help me." And Jesus answered and said to her, "Martha, Martha, you are worried and troubled about many things. But one thing is needed, and Mary has chosen that good part, which will not be taken away from her."*

There is something powerful about going into 'the secret place' to commune with God. This is a quiet retreat into His presence, unseen by the outside world, without any desire to be recognised by others as being especially devoted. Here, the deepest concerns of the heart are shared, spiritual barriers are battled through and the liberating truth and guidance of God Himself is encountered. Quality time spent in secret, with an audience of just One, brings untold benefits to our life lived in the open, and for His kingdom on earth.

Matt. 6:5-6:

> *"And when you pray, you shall not be like the hypocrites. For they love to pray standing in the synagogues and on the corners of the streets, that they may be seen by men. Assuredly, I say to you, they have their reward. But you, when you pray, go into your room, and when you have shut your door, pray to your Father who is in the secret place; and your Father who sees in secret will reward you openly."*

I like watching sports on TV (probably too much if you ask my wife). Football, rugby, cricket, tennis, even darts – there's usually something on at any time during the week that piques my interest! One thing struck me whilst watching an athletics championship recently. Admiring the fine performance of one of the athletes, the commentator and expert pundit mentioned how all the key work in training had been done for weeks and months prior to the event, and that on the day itself she was able to relax and let all the hard preparation click into place and manifest as an impressive, and deceptively effortless, victory. It reminded me of how, if we are to be overcomers in a pressurised world, we need to be regularly spending time before the Lord, paying the price of commitment, to be properly trained and equipped.

2) <u>All the time</u>

1 Thess. 5:16-18:

> *Rejoice always, pray without ceasing, in everything give thanks; for this is the will of God in Christ Jesus for you.*

The Lord Jesus Christ had a most remarkable relationship with His Father in that there was a constant interaction and obedience with Him that characterised His entire life; the book of John provides an illuminating portrayal of this intimate relationship (see 5:19-20, 30; 6:38; 8:28-29, 38; 12:49-50; 14:10, 31).

The reality of the indwelling Holy Spirit in the life of a believer means that we are enabled to have constant communion with Him as we go through our daily business. We have the privilege of bringing Him into all the situations of life that we find ourselves in, continuously being open to His wisdom and strength in all matters. Routine, mundane activities can be transformed into moments of worship and drawing near to His throne of grace. This is the life of abiding in Him, like the branches of a life-giving vine (Jn. 15:4-5).

3) Special times

There will be times and occasions where we need to spend a particularly focused and extended period of time with God; this may be in order to seek clarity about important decisions or to wrestle through an especially challenging situation. Examples of this include lengthy prayer walks, overnight prayer, spiritual retreats etc.

It is vital that we don't separate specific and special times with the Lord from the continual walk with Him as we go about our daily business; each of these things feed into and facilitate each other. We must not reduce our relationship with God to a set time of the day or particular defined period and then live the rest of the time in our own strength and for our own purposes.

Means of grace

The means of grace are spiritual activities that can help us cultivate and maintain a close walk with God. They are not just for individual but are for corporate practice; God's design is that we grow in community. I give a brief description here[2]:

1) Worship

This is the turning of our hearts to Almighty God in gratitude, consecration and awe. It is a humble recognition of His absolute worthiness. There are special times of worship on your own or in community (church) but in one sense, worship is the entire Christian life (Rom. 12:1). Worship goes hand-in-hand with thanksgiving for what He has done and praise for who He is.

2) Prayer

This is the life-breath of the Christian life. It is two-way communication with the living God who hears and speaks. Prayer can be both natural and spontaneous as well as structured and well thought out beforehand.

Again, the Holy Spirit Himself helps us to pray (Rom. 8:26; Eph. 6:18 etc.) such that our prayers are in keeping with His will. This includes the disciplines of silence and solitude where we are comfortably alone with our own thoughts whilst coming into His presence.

3) The Word of God

His Word is truth and food for our souls (Matt. 4:4 etc.). It is not just head knowledge but life giving truth that stirs our souls, challenges us and moulds us into His likeness (2 Tim. 3:16). Faith comes by hearing, and hearing by the Word of God (Rom. 10:17).

There are different ways of learning the Word. Some sort of system of reading through and studying the Bible is very valuable but should not become a legalistic endeavour.

Not everyone is going to be a good reader; listening to the Word can be very helpful and in this day and age there are plenty of high-quality audio/video resources that can be readily accessed through various forms of technology.

Journaling can be a helpful exercise in terms of capturing insights and crystallising thoughts. The practice of memorising and meditating on Scripture has benefited many.

4) Community

God desires that we grow in community with other believers and He gives us the privilege to do so by placing us in the body of Christ. God has a master plan of building a new community centred in Jesus and lasting for all eternity in order to reflect His glory (Eph. 3:14-21).

We are adopted into a new family through what Jesus has done for us. Hence we have a relationship as sons and daughters with a loving Father, who receives us and does not judge us. 'Life is relationships, the rest is just details'[3].

The call is now to live in blessed community in a way that truly glorifies God (Ecc. 4:9-12; Acts 2:42-47; Rom. 12:3-13; Gal. 6:2; Eph. 4:15-16; Phil. 2:3-16; Heb. 10:24-25; 1 Pet. 2:9-10). The love and unity of believers is a powerful witness to the unsaved world (Jn. 13:34-35; Ps. 133).

As we begin to think in terms of community, we move away from potentially self-centred individualism towards a spirit of 'one anothering' within a body of believers[4]. We thus harness the tremendous power of community, the way it was meant to be. This includes practical help and support for each other as well as spiritual encouragement through conversations and connection at a deeper level.

The sense of belonging and identity, practical support, mutual encouragement etc. can all have a positive impact on a person's mental health and overall functioning.

5) Outreach

A believer who has been touched by the grace of God cannot help but want to share His love and truth with others, both non-believers and other followers of Christ. A life of self-giving service is a privilege and joy; I cover more on this in the next section.

6) Discipline

The ability to lead disciplined lives characterised by appropriate self-control is truly a gift. We can take charge of ourselves, assume necessary responsibility and exercise healthy authority. This includes developing a life of order with a clear sense of power, purpose and planning. It also involves the freedom that comes from simplicity and not being too tied to material things.

God also lovingly disciplines and trains us through trials that refine and build character. We need not be afraid of this because He surely knows what He is doing and has our best interests in mind.

7) Celebration

The Christian life is not just about seriousness and weighty matters. There is a place for fun and joy, feasting and celebration. When we consider how good and gracious God is, what other response is appropriate? It is telling that some of us have to deliberately remind ourselves and make particular effort to wholeheartedly rejoice in what He has already done and not just be seeking after a deeper experience of Him.

A note on terminology. Some people refer to the above practices as 'spiritual disciplines' which is of course a helpful description. I prefer the term 'means of grace', for two reasons. *Means* reminds us that they are but a means to an end i.e. to know God better. *Grace* reminds us that we are dependent on His empowering if we are to engage in them effectively and derive the benefit that they are designed to bring.

If we lose sight of this, we can end up trying harder to perform spiritually without actually coming into a closer relationship with Him, and end up rather frustrated, disillusioned and even cynical about the things of God.

A life of service

The call to serve

Gal. 5:13:

> *For you, brethren, have been called to liberty; only do not use liberty as an opportunity for the flesh, but through love serve one another.*

Jesus Himself provides the best example of servant leadership i.e. using our position and power in Christ for sacrificial service that God may be known and glorified. Jn. 13:14-15:

> *"If I then, your Lord and Teacher, have washed your feet, you also ought to wash one another's feet. For I have given you an example, that you should do as I have done to you."*

If we truly realise how wonderful the gospel is, the natural step is to share it with others in humble service. We have something really good to tell others! When our own needs are fully met in Christ, we are enabled to live an outward-focused life of love and service to others; we serve not to impress but because of a heart that is full to overflowing.

Areas of service

Matt. 28:18-20:

> *And Jesus came and spoke to them, saying, "All authority has been given to Me in heaven and on earth. Go therefore and make disciples of all the nations, baptising them in the name of the Father and of the Son and of the Holy Spirit, teaching them to observe all things that I have commanded*

you; and lo, I am with you always, even to the end of the age."

The great commission is about the service of making disciples, not just converts. This involves evangelism (of non-believers) and discipleship (of believers). As we have been seeing, not only does the gospel have the power to bring someone into the kingdom of God but it has the ability to keep someone in it and bring them to maturity in Christ.

Consider service in several different areas:

1) Sharing Christ with non-believers

We are called and empowered for a ministry of outreach/evangelism (Acts. 1:8). God has designed it such that He uses humans to convey His key message, and that His gospel spreads from person to person. Mission (both near neighbour and global) is the heartbeat of Christianity; God is a missionary God.

Our evangelism is backed up by the assurance that God is indeed drawing people to Himself and has been at work in their lives even before we meet and speak with them. Our task is to discern where and how He is moving and cooperate with what He is doing in the work of salvation. We also need to pray that veils of darkness be removed so that they can see the light.

2) Serving other believers/the church

God supplies gifts to the church for mutual benefit and building up the body of Christ within the church. There is much joy in seeing the Spirit at work within a community of believers, bringing truth, healing and deliverance to the followers of Christ (1 Cor. 12; Rom. 12; Eph. 4; I Pet. 4:11).

As we serve one another, multiplicative discipleship is facilitated whereby there can be 'exponential cascading' of the life and truth of Christ. In this way, the church grows both wide and deep, with the corresponding growth in community and the mental health benefits that that brings.

3) <u>Service to the whole world</u>

I have heard one accusation levelled against Christians that they can be 'too heavenly minded to be of any earthly use'. (Mind you, I have heard someone reply 'I don't want to be so earthly minded as to be of no heavenly use'!) Nevertheless, the point is that the Christian's hope in Christ should lead them to be valuable citizens of this world who are endeavouring to 'make the world a better place'.

Christians should not be lazy or aloof and overly spiritual to the point that they seem to be contributing little for the wider benefit of society; there is a rightful place for innovative creativity, hard work, and rightful praise for worthy achievements.

We have the privilege and opportunity to be a blessing wherever we are and go be it in our family, workplace, church, sporting club etc., shining the light of Christ in places that may not have seen this before. There are many opportunities to serve the community at large and in so doing we reflect the love of Christ to a hurting and needy world, to the poor and marginalised.

Freedom and joy in service

In His marvellous ways, not only are we given the privilege of serving Him and others and empowered to do so, a life of service can bring much freedom and joy personally. It is a beautiful cycle of grace: we are blessed to bless others and in so doing receive more blessing ourselves.

For Christians, one of the greatest joys in life is seeing someone else come to Christ. There is joy in the presence of the angels of God over one sinner who repents (Lk. 15:10)! There seems to be a special grace present whenever we step out in faith and proclaim His kingdom to a lost world.

I find that everyday life and work becomes much more doable when I can realign my thinking with the real reason I am doing what I am doing. When things feel more burdensome and draining, I seek to remind myself that my life is His and that I am here to serve Him and others in His strength, and that my life is not all about me.

Acts 20:35:

> *"I have shown you in every way, by labouring like this, that you must support the weak. And remember the words of the Lord Jesus, that He said, 'It is more blessed to give than to receive.'"*

Chapter 8

CONCLUSION

Summary of main points

We began by outlining the vision of the book; then the need of the world and the fact that Christianity has real answers. We then defined the vision statement in more detail i.e. what is meant by the gospel, mental health and the relationship between the two.

We saw how the gospel is primarily about God and how His infinite love and unwavering justice are both fulfilled at Calvary. Through what He has done, sinful man can be reconciled with a holy God. Judgement against sin is satisfied, broken relationships can be made new. A fallen world is now on course for glorious restoration in the age to come.

All the blessings of the gospel flow from the willing sacrifice of the Lord Jesus Christ. The inner peace that comes from a right standing with God. The power to live that is available through the indwelling Holy Spirit. The prospect of an eternity spent in the glorious presence of God. And, here and now, a mind that can grow in health and maturity.

The following table summarises the truths of the gospel and the ways in which they can bring benefit to the mental health of a believer:

Gospel truths	Application that can potentially benefit a believer's mental health
It's all about Him God reveals Himself through His Word • There is a God • He has revealed Himself as great, good, holy • He created us to know Him and made a way for us to do so	*We can come to know a God who is good* • *We can know Him personally* • *The big pieces fall into place* • *Our faith is in a God who is just*
God is the centre of the universe • God is the essence and pinnacle of all existence • All things exist for His glory; worship is the appropriate response • We were created to be utterly dependent on Him	*We can place Him first in our lives* • *We can come into right alignment with how things were made to be* • *Putting Him first is a real privilege* • *Putting Him first can bring much relief and joy!*
God is working out His purposes for all creation • The great big picture • His sovereignty and power to work it out • This extends to a personal level; He draws us to Himself	*We can be assured of His working in our lives* • *From selfish stuckness to Spirit-led sanctification* • *No more excessive striving (even as Christians)* • *The value of our journeys*

The gift of brokenness	
We live in a broken world	*We can assume appropriate responsibility for our problems*
<ul><li>This is not hard to see</li><li>The Bible presents a coherent explanation</li><li>Thankfully, the story doesn't end there</li></ul>	<ul><li>*An accurate view of the reasons for our difficulties*</li><li>*Appropriate responsibility-taking*</li><li>*There is true hope when the real issues can be tackled*</li></ul>
Our sin is a major problem	*A sin paradigm enables a Saviour solution*
<ul><li>A focus on one key area</li><li>The potential impact of sin on mental health</li><li>This sets us up for salvation through a Saviour</li></ul>	<ul><li>*The helpfulness of thinking about sin*</li><li>*The need and ability for genuine repentance*</li><li>*The danger of excluding a sin paradigm*</li></ul>
God allows us to have a sense of our own brokenness	*Brokenness can be a gateway to grace*
<ul><li>A vision of His ways</li><li>Defining brokenness</li><li>He brings us to the end of ourselves for His glory and our benefit</li></ul>	<ul><li>*There can be great blessing in our brokenness and pain*</li><li>*How does this work in practice?*</li><li>*A story of redemption*</li></ul>
What Jesus has done	
His death, burial and resurrection makes a way for us to have right standing before God	*In Christ, we can have acceptance before performance*

<ul><li>The crux of the matter</li><li>The double blessing</li><li>This is utterly radical</li></ul>	<ul><li>*Acceptance before performance*</li><li>*Two potentially helpful applications*</li><li>*'Good enough for now'*</li></ul>
We are adopted into the family of God<ul><li>God thinks bigger than just individuals</li><li>We become His children</li><li>The church becomes our family</li></ul>	*We can experience the blessings of a new family in Christ*<ul><li>*The impact of families on our upbringing*</li><li>*The church can come into its own in this area*</li><li>*A reality check*</li></ul>
We have a model of true forgiveness<ul><li>Jesus provides the supreme example</li><li>An analysis of forgiveness</li><li>He calls and enables us to walk in forgiveness</li></ul>	*We can live in the freedom that forgiveness brings*<ul><li>*We have the power to forgive*</li><li>*Some key applications to mental health/ wellbeing*</li><li>*'Perpetual fresh starts'*</li></ul>
Power to change The Holy Spirit indwells and empowers us<ul><li>General introduction to the Holy Spirit</li><li>Brief survey of the Holy Spirit in the Old and New Testaments</li><li>The experience of the Holy Spirit for present day believers</li></ul>	*We have a new power to live and change*<ul><li>*Fundamental inner change*</li><li>*Divine strategy for issues faced*</li><li>*A particular application to the area of stress and anxiety*</li></ul>

We are called to holiness	*We have the privilege of experiencing the joy of holiness*
<ul><li>What is holiness?</li><li>The call to holiness</li><li>The ability to be holy</li></ul>	<ul><li>*The joy of holiness*</li><li>*Pathways to holiness*</li><li>*Divine cooperation*</li></ul>
We enter into real spiritual conflict	*The experience of spiritual conflict can strengthen our character*
<ul><li>The reality of spiritual warfare</li><li>The enemies of our soul</li><li>Fighting from a place of victory</li></ul>	<ul><li>*Knowing where the battle is*</li><li>*Spiritual warfare can be character-building*</li><li>*Towards maturity*</li></ul>
<u>Eternal perspective</u>	
This world is passing away, and a better reality is to come	*We can have a pilgrim mentality whilst on this earth*
<ul><li>The reality of Christian eschatology (or 'the study of last things')</li><li>The nature of Christian eschatology</li><li>Unity (in diversity) in eschatology</li></ul>	<ul><li>*Our temporary passage*</li><li>*Not too attached to this world*</li><li>*Open-handed living*</li></ul>
God brings strength, meaning and hope in the midst of trials and tribulations	*We can experience the grace to endure difficulty*
<ul><li>The reality of pain and suffering</li><li>The Bible presents a robust view of suffering</li><li>In Christ, there is</li></ul>	<ul><li>He supplies grace in adversity</li><li>Components of grace for trials</li><li>Refiner's fire</li></ul>

strength, meaning and hope for those who suffer	
We are destined to rule and reign with Him	*Our lives now are a preparation for future work in His kingdom*
<ul><li>A glorious future awaits</li><li>Specific work to be done</li><li>Preparation for what is ahead</li></ul>	<ul><li>What we do now really matters</li><li>Fully alive in all situations</li><li>The worthy goal of maturity</li></ul>

<u>**Our response**</u>

> Core responses: the 'always attitudes'

- What they are
- Why they are necessary
- Altogether, all the time, by His power

> Cultivating a close walk with the Lord

- He helps us with this
- Rhythms of communion with God
  - Means of grace

> A life of service

- The call to serve
- Areas of service
- Freedom and joy in service

Relationship to mental health areas: in Chapter 1, I outlined five areas which, if there is wellbeing and growth in them, good mental health can ensue. In the table below, I try and link how the gospel truths and applications described in this book can collectively have a positive impact in each of these areas:

Area of mental health	How the gospel can potentially have a positive impact on this area
Thoughts, feelings and behaviours	*These can be undergirded by the truth of God's Word and empowered by God's Spirit such that the nature of our mind, emotions and actions can be characterised by wisdom and grace leading to peace (and not anxiety) and hope (and not depression).*
Relationships	*We can enter into new and fulfilling relationships with God, ourselves and others. We are able to relate well with ourselves because of the acceptance, without prior performance, that can be found in Christ. We have the privilege of experiencing a new family where the love and nurture of God can be manifested. We are provided with the grace to be able to relate well to others on the basis of being so secure within ourselves and having a robust model of forgiveness through what Jesus has done on the cross.*
Level of day-to-day functioning	*We can depend on Him for the very motivation and strength to get out of bed each day, look after ourselves well and contribute as best as we can to society. He also provides specific calling and gifting such that we have a place to serve and flourish within the body of Christ. Our daily work can become of value for all eternity.*

Resilience (including conflict resolution)	*The gospel does not shirk from the harsh realities of life in a fallen world. Disciples of Christ are both called to and equipped for suffering in this world. In the midst of trials and tribulations, He supplies strength, meaning and hope. We are enabled to boldly and honestly resolve conflict within the framework of His grace and love.*
Character and maturity	*The gospel is about redemption from small-minded, self-centred living, to sacrificial, Christlike godliness. He is actively seeking to build character and maturity in our lives. We are privileged to be partakers of this and to experience the joy of holiness and purity and reap the benefits of a life lived well in Christ.*

A key message to be left with

In this book, I have tried to explain the gospel clearly and make a particular application of it to the area of mental health/wellbeing, in order to show believers what a full-orbed and transformational message they have in the good news of Jesus Christ.

On a very real and practical level, my desire is that Christians will truly learn and experience the tremendous blessing that God had prepared for them in Christ, to be able to walk in the fullness of the Holy Spirit moment-by-moment (what I call 'living full in the moment'). In this way of living the truths of the gospel converge on one moment in time and empower the believer to know Him and make Him known each step of the way throughout the day.

It is not a head-in-the-clouds, superficial approach to the complexity of life but rather a full engagement with it, enabled by the security of being in Him, the wisdom of knowing how to approach each situation and the God-given resilience to persevere through difficulty when this is required.

It is my earnest prayer that the contents of this book will help the follower of Christ to live in His fullness as much as possible, all the days of his/her life.

Col. 2:6-7:

> *As you therefore have received Christ Jesus the Lord, so walk in Him, rooted and built up in Him and established in the faith, as you have been taught, abounding in it with thanksgiving.*

Gal. 5:16-18:

> *I say then: Walk in the Spirit, and you shall not fulfil the lust of the flesh. For the flesh lusts against the Spirit, and the Spirit against the flesh; and these are contrary to one another, so that you do not do the things that you wish. But if you are led by the Spirit, you are not under the law.*

Some final words

We have covered a lot of ground in these chapters and it will no doubt take time to digest the material and allow it to have a positive experiential impact on your life. Don't be in any hurry to grow but stay focused on the Lord and He will direct your paths. The journey itself is as important as the destination.

In this book, we have but scratched the surface of a gospel that is infinitely rich in truth and meaning. My hope is that this has been just the start of a journey, and that from here, under the tutelage of the Holy Spirit Himself, you will learn more and more about His wonderful grace as it applies to all areas of life.

This is an earnest prayer:

"Be blessed
As you seek Him
and come to know Him
through His glorious gospel
May your mind be healthy and strong
May you find true personal freedom in Christ."

Appendix A

Who this book is for

I have the following groups in mind:

<u>For Christians</u>

This book has been written primarily for those who have already become believers in and followers of Christ and who are actively seeking to grow in their faith. I have sought to be interdenominational in approach, focusing on the core theological concepts and orthodox beliefs that can unite Christians rather than divide them.

It will hopefully be of use to Christians who are struggling with various problems of living. This is not a diagnostic tool or self-help manual but a reminder and guide to what a follower of Christ already believes or what they need to realise about the faith which they have embraced.

It also aims to help believers have a good 'baseline' level of mental wellbeing such that future major problems could potentially be averted.

I am seeking to encourage Christians who are specifically wanting to utilise the resources of God in their ongoing journey of growth and transformation; I am wanting to help them realise the key points of this approach which is centred on:

1) God

The focus is on God Himself for whose glory all things exist. We are to look to Him for freedom and not to man. We have His resources at our disposal – His Word, His Spirit, His people. My goal is to point people to God as their ultimate source of help, not to anyone else or anything else in His place.

2) Gospel

The method of change presented here is based explicitly on the gospel, the great redemptive story which runs through the whole Bible. Jesus Christ is the pivotal figure. This involves an approach that can seem counterintuitive, where the way up is down, where strength comes through weakness.

3) Grace

The gospel is a message saturated with grace, the lavish provision of undeserved favour. We are accepted and made right with God by grace through faith (Eph. 2:8). The Holy Spirit supplies daily wisdom and strength that we may be overcomers in all that He has called us to be and do.

4) Growth

The goal is maturity. The gospel is the way in which God transforms sinful man into Christlike disciples. As long as we are on the journey, moving with the right trajectory of growth and aiming to move forwards in our lives, we can rest assured that we are walking faithfully with Him ('it's the direction we are travelling in, not the distance travelled, that matters').

A note to seekers

It may be that someone has picked up this book because they are seeking truth and answers to questions which they have yet to find anywhere else. It may be that the Spirit of God Himself has been drawing you to a personal knowledge of Him through the realisation of your own desperate need for a Saviour and a life lived right with God. It is sincerely hoped that here in this book you will find a clear explanation of the gospel so that you can be ready to make an appropriate response.

If you are seeking further information and understanding about the gospel, the following books may be of benefit to you (in addition to some other books listed in the 'Further Resources' chapter):

- Graham, B. (2012). *Peace with God: The secret of happiness.* Thomas Nelson
- Gumbel, N. (2010). *Questions of life.* Alpha International
- Stanley, A. (2005). *How good is good enough?* Multnomah Press

If you are in a position to make a faith response at this point, the following prayer may help you express this to God Himself:

"Dear God,

I now understand the gospel better. I realise that it is all about Your great plan to restore all of creation for Your glory and to bring sinful man back to a close relationship with You.

I realise my need. I acknowledge my sin, and how I have lived my own way, in my own strength for so long. I repent from this, and turn away from a self-centred, self-directed life. I want to live for You.

I believe that Jesus Christ died and rose again so that the penalty of my sin can be paid for on my behalf. I joyfully accept the fact that by faith, His goodness becomes my goodness such that I can be fully accepted and valued in Your sight.

I understand that the Holy Spirit wants to live in and direct the lives of all believers. I ask to be filled with the Holy Spirit and that I experience

---

the abundant life that you desire for me.

I thank you that you have a glorious future prepared for Your people and that my eternal destiny is secure in You.

I commit to a life of repentance, faith, surrender and obedience as You enable me to respond in this way. I desire to walk close with You all the days of my life that I may serve You faithfully and bring all glory and honour to Your name.

Thank you for Your amazing grace.

Amen."

If you have made this prayerful response, speak to somebody who you know is a committed Christian and tell them about it.

This is just the start of a lifelong journey of growth in God which will be full of discovery and challenges, though in my opinion it is the best path to be on. Praying a one-off sincere prayer is a significant first step but is by no means all it takes to become and live as a Christian. Like a couple who are devoted to each other: the wedding is great and should be celebrated but it is the lifelong marriage that is important.

Seek out a vibrant, Bible-believing church where you can be gradually discipled and learn to follow Christ over time, alongside a wider community of fellow believers.

A note to non-believers (and sceptics)

This book will no doubt be highly controversial to a non-believer, particularly one who is sceptical of faith matters. As can be seen, it is explicitly Christian and makes all the presuppositions associated with traditional Christian faith. The message of the gospel itself is intensely radical and often offensive: it dethrones human beings from the position of supreme authority in personal issues and calls people to humble themselves before a mighty God; this is a major insult to human pride.

But I in no way want to antagonise or insult the intelligence of genuine non-believers/sceptics who are sincerely seeking truth. I have a lot of respect for science and the scientific method. My view is that faith and science are not incompatible, although their relationship has to be carefully thought through.

I take the 'all truth is God's truth' approach i.e. science is the rigorous and systematic discovery of God's creation, for increase in understanding of what really is and the practical advancement of society; Christians can and should be very much part of this noble endeavour.

It is beyond the scope of this book to present a comprehensive apologetic for the Christian faith and engage in fuller discussion about this. For those interested in gaining more information, the following books may be helpful:

- Glass, D. H. (2012). *Atheism's new clothes.* Apollos
- Keller, T. (2009). *The reason for God.* Hodder & Stoughton
- Lennox, J. C. (2011). *Seven days that divide the world.* Zondervan
- Lewis, C. S. (2012). *Mere Christianity (C. S. Lewis Signature Classic).* William Collins
- McDowell, J. (2010). *New evidence that demands a verdict.* Thomas Nelson
- Strobel, L. (1998). *The case for Christ.* Zondervan

The following ministries/websites may also be helpful:

- Bethinking.org (www.bethinking.org)
- Centre for Public Christianity (www.publicchristianity.org)
- Oxford Centre for Christian Apologetics (www.theocca.org)
- Reasonable Faith (www.reasonablefaith.org)

- Saints & Sceptics (www.saintsandsceptics.org)
- Unbelievable?
  (www.premierchristianradio.com/unbelievable)

Note: these books/ministries may not so much convince others as they do strengthen the faith of believers themselves and assure them that their faith is founded on fact and reasonable evidence and is not far-fetched and unfounded as some would lead us to believe. It is vital that we are always ready to give a defence to everyone who asks us a reason for the hope that is in us (1 Pet. 3:15).

Appendix B

How this book could be used

There are several points to consider:

General points

There is a lot of material covered in this book but mainly in a broad, panoramic, overview fashion; each subsection has been/could be the basis for separate books in themselves! There is obviously scope for further study and the resources at the back of the book point to additional relevant material.

This book can of course be used for individual study and devotional reflection. In this case, it may be helpful to read through it once and then return to particular chapters or topics that seem most relevant to your particular life situation.

It may be useful as a basis for small group study or discussion. In this case, it would be necessary for the group facilitator(s) to be familiar with the material contained herein and in particular the vision of using it to provide helpful foundational truth, without an expectation that it will solve all the problems that people present with.

It could potentially be helpful to Christians who are in pastoral counselling roles both informally or more formally, and be used as one source of information that can help integrate a person's faith with their everyday struggles in a hopefully practical and effective manner.

Specific applications

The truths and applications of the gospel laid out here will hopefully be of help to Christians who are struggling with various problems in living which have been difficult to cope with and which negatively affect their daily lives. The material can of course be supplemented by other Christ-centred materials and approaches depending on the difficulties that are being faced.

Additional benefit may be added if such a person were to work through the contents of the book with a committed friend/pastoral carer who can provide support and encouragement throughout the process. The material is not just theoretical but can be lived out and applied in everyday life and to that end, there is great value in learning and growing together in loving community.

The contents of this book are in no way a substitute for professional help or scientifically-established treatments for clearly defined and recognised mental illnesses/disorders when these are necessary.

A 'primer for discipleship'

I see freedom in Christ as being very much part of the overall vision of discipleship and pastoral care within the local church.

Hence, this book may be usefully incorporated into a structured discipleship programme, or be taught as a discrete short course within a church setting as part of continuing Christian education.

It could potentially be viewed as a 'primer' for Christian discipleship as I believe it lays out the key aspects of the gospel, which is the main story that Christians need to become intimately familiar with both intellectually and experientially in their journey of growth. The truths and their applications are 'timeless' in that they are always relevant to a believer's walk with God, no matter what their stage of maturity. It can also help to build a consistency of belief and approach within a particular congregation, as these fundamental truths are shared and lived out in united community.

I would be very keen that this content can be used in a preventative way, i.e. by establishing in Christians a 'baseline' understanding and experience of the power of the gospel even before trouble comes their way. In this way, they can potentially be better prepared to cope and overcome whenever the inevitable difficulties of life arise.

Appendix C

The interface with mental health services

Here are some thoughts about the interface of gospel-centred approaches to helping people who are struggling and established mental health services (with reference to the UK system[1]) and indeed to scientific psychology/psychiatry[2] in general:

This is not a 'turf war' book

The basic 'genre' of this book is the biblical counselling movement that has and is producing a growing literature on tackling human problems through explicitly gospel-centred approaches. This mainly took off in the USA in the 1960s and 1970s and was sparked by a seminal publication by a reformed pastor called Jay Adams – *Competent to counsel*[3].

Since then, organisations such as The Christian Counselling and Educational Foundation (CCEF)[4], the Biblical Counselling Coalition (BCC)[5] and the Association of Certified Biblical Counsellors (ACBC)[6] have emerged to take forward this approach. More recently, a UK-based network, Biblical Counselling UK (BCUK) has emerged[7].

In the earlier days, there was an attempt to 'reclaim' the care/cure of souls to the church. There were some leaders who would regard with some suspicion the secular approaches to helping people as found in secular psychology/psychiatry. In some places, a 'turf war' resulted which at times became quite heated and controversial.

This is not my approach here. I am not trying to subvert the mental health system or create an alternative approach to some of the conditions and problems which have been extensively studied and for which effective treatment approaches have been developed and positively evaluated. Where indicated, sufferers should not be deprived of treatments that are known to relieve suffering and aid recovery.

A collaborative, complementary model

I am in favour of Christians and churches having a collaborative, complementary model when it comes to mental health services and psychology/psychiatry. This means that when someone might/would benefit from help within that field, they should be supported in getting it. If possible attempts should be made to collaborate with services such that churches can understand what treatment their members are getting, and also explain what resources they can provide from a pastoral care and supportive community point of view. Potential conflicts in role and approach can then hopefully be identified and worked upon in the best possible way.

There are some instances where it is very clear that professional mental health services should be accessed (and it would be unwise for Christians/the church to try and manage these problems on their own). These usually involve people who have more serious mental illness e.g. schizophrenia, bipolar affective disorder, severe depressive/anxiety disorders, severe eating/personality disorders, major substance misuse, autistic spectrum disorder, dementia etc.

As a general principle, the church needs to refer whenever there are significant issues to do with:

1) <u>Physiology</u>

The conditions mentioned above are characterised by significant biological contributions to their cause as well as the potential for severe physical complications. There are other medical conditions that may cause mental health problems (organic injury, hormonal disturbance, some forms of cancer etc.). Medication could be the mainstay of treatment for some of the above and physical/medical monitoring is essential in some instances. The church itself is not equipped to assess and manage conditions for which proper physical assessment is required.

2) <u>Risk</u>

Patients who are at significant risk to themselves or others as a result of their mental health condition need to be properly assessed and managed by trained professionals working within systems that can help manage and contain this risk. At the extreme end some patients will require full inpatient care, and even continuous nursing supervision to help them remain safe during a period of crisis where risk is extremely high.

3) <u>Resources/systems</u>

Some patients require a comprehensive, multidisciplinary team around them to address their complex needs and support their recovery (e.g. psychiatrist, mental health nurse, social worker, occupational therapist, psychologist, general practitioner etc. all working together). Such service provision requires a coordinated, well functioning system with clear pathways of care. The church would be unable to provide this kind of comprehensive professional care.

Mental health professionals within churches can have a useful and important role to play in helping to triage people within their congregation and help to decide whether they need referral into the mental health system[8].

They can also help to improve collaboration between the church and mental health system, in part by helping the believer/church to navigate the system and understand how it works.

Some specific issues

There are some issues that Christians might find particularly problematic in relation to psychology/psychiatry and how it might conflict with their faith. I offer some thoughts about these although in no way are these full or final comments on the topics.

1) Diagnosis

Some people may find it problematic being labelled a certain way. They may believe it takes away from their identity as a redeemed child of God and may lead to unnecessary stigma particularly within environments where there is less understanding about mental health issues.

On the other hand, diagnoses can be very useful and give meaning and sense to the patient's experience, as well as the encouragement that they are not alone in their suffering, and that their condition has and is being actively studied and researched.

Perhaps of some concern is when everyday problems of living are overmedicalised with the (conscious/unconscious) intention of avoiding personal responsibility and underlying issues in the hope that external solutions (e.g. medication only) will fix the problem.

2) Medication[9]

Some Christians may be reluctant to take recommended medication out of a fear of side-effects but also in the belief that to do so would be a sign of weakness and lack of faith in God. This would be an unfortunate situation if the medication was genuinely required for a particular treatable condition.

In essence, if a mental health diagnosis has been made by a

trained professional and medication felt to be in the best interests of the patient, as long as the medication is being properly prescribed and monitored, the Christians should adhere to this advice.

This does not mean that he/she doesn't question it if it seems to be causing problematic side effects or is not being effective but they should not make a unilateral decision to stop medication because of their own faith beliefs or only on the advice of a pastoral carer.

3) Therapy[10]

The issue of psychological therapy might be a bit trickier as there is more potential for clash in beliefs and philosophies in terms of overarching worldview and underlying operating principles. There could be a particular conflict in relation to the gist of how people change i.e. whether or not the power to change ultimately comes from within or from above.

Having said that, a Christian should seriously consider taking up a period of psychological treatment if it has been recommended by a qualified healthcare professional who has made a thorough assessment of their condition, as they can stand to benefit at some level.

This also raises the question as to whether Christians should refer themselves to a secular therapist in their search for help. Again, this can be very helpful, particular with a skilled therapist who will not be antagonistic to their faith.

It is important to bear in mind that the symptomatic benefits of seeing a good counsellor/therapist can be immense, and can place people in a better position to engage with and further explore their faith.

My own view is that professional counselling/therapy could potentially run alongside good pastoral counselling/care as long as there can be a clear differentiation of role/focus on both sides.

Ideally, there will be some collaboration between those who are trying to help the individual, in order to ensure that there are no mixed messages and confusion in terms of what is being addressed and worked on in sessions.

Endnotes

1. <u>Introduction</u>

1. Particularly when success in Christian leadership is assumed due to large numbers of followers and slick presentation.

2. The Mental Health Foundation (www.mentalhealth.org.uk) provides some useful statistics on mental health conditions and issues.

3. The Samaritans Suicide Statistics Report 2014 (www.samaritans.org/sites/default/files/kcfinder/files/research/Samaritans%20Suicide%20Statistics%20Report%202014.pdf).

4. One succinct description of the gospel storyline is: Creation. Fall. Redemption.

5. I believe salvation should be viewed as being a lifelong process rather than a one-off event i.e. Christians are people who have been saved (justification), are being saved (sanctification) and will be saved (glorification) from sin and all its insidious effects.

6. Wimber, J. (2006). *The way in is the way on*. Ampelon Publishing.

7. The two current main classification manuals for mental disorders are: World Health Organization. (1992). *The ICD-10 classification of mental and behavioural disorders* and American Psychiatric Association. (2013). *Diagnostic and statistical manual of mental disorders: Fifth edition (DSM-5)*. (The ICD-10 is due to be updated to ICD-11 in the foreseeable future.)

8. The term 'existential crisis' has been used to describe 'a

moment at (or period during) which an individual questions the very foundation of his/her life, whether it has any meaning, purpose or value'.

9. www.who.int/features/factfiles/mental_health/en/index.html (accessed 28/9/14).

10. For example the work of positive psychologists such as Mihaly Csikszentmihalyi where 'flow' is defined as 'the mental state of operation in which a person performing an activity is fully immersed in a feeling of energised focus, full involvement, and enjoyment in the process of the activity. In essence, flow is characterised by complete absorption in what one does.'

11. Ortberg, J. (2014). *Soulkeeping.* Zondervan. This helpful book is set in the context of Pastor Ortberg's mentoring relationship with Professor Willard and provides a summary of some of the key lessons that he learnt from him over the years.

12. Some of the more well-known stories are those of paraplegic Joni Eareckson Tada and Nick Vujicic (an Australian Christian evangelist and motivational speaker born with tetra-amelia syndrome, a rare disorder characterised by the absence of all four limbs) as well as the suffering saints of old. But it is the many untold stories of faithful perseverance that happen in congregations all over the world, each and every day, that really impress me.

2. It's all about Him

1. Grudem, W. (1994). *Systematic theology: An introduction to Biblical doctrine.* IVP

2. A phrase attributed to Blaise Pascal (1623-1662) from his quote, *'There is a God-shaped vacuum in the heart of every man which cannot be filled by any created thing, but only by God, the Creator, made known through Jesus.'*

3. The work of Andrew Newberg would be a good place to start (www.andrewnewberg.com).

4. www.kevinhalloran.net/best-c-s-lewis-quotes (accessed 28/9/14).

5. www.crosswalk.com/blogs/tchividjian/the-supremacy-of-christ-11610734.html (accessed 28/9/14).

6. Kidd, S. M. (2006). *When the heart waits.* HarperCollins.

7. Keller, T. (2012). *The freedom of self-forgetfulness.* 10Publishing.

8. It's so important to be able to see the gospel as being much more than an individualistic experience, and to remind ourselves that our story fits into a much, much bigger one.

9. Sproul, R. C. (2005). *Chosen by God.* Tyndale House Publishers.

10. So-called 'third wave' cognitive behavioural therapies that are being increasingly empirically supported as treatment for a range of mental health conditions.

3. <u>The gift of brokenness</u>

1. It can be difficult to distinguish between the interrelated concepts of guilt and shame. One simplified way of describing them is guilt – 'I have done something bad/ wrong' and shame – 'I am bad/wrong'.

2. There will be understandable difficulties with this concept in the mind of those who have not come under the revelatory conviction of the Holy Spirit as regards personal brokenness. How can this be fair? What hope do we then have if we are dysfunctional at the core, right from the outset? Thankfully the story does not end here and whilst we all inherit sin from one man, grace and transformation have been made freely available through another Man (Rom. 5:12-21).

3. Adams, J. (1970). *Competent to counsel: Introduction to nouthetic counselling.* Zondervan.

4. I am not advocating some sort of spiritual masochism but there really can be a strange, liberating blessing that comes when we surrender our utter helplessness to the Lord in the moment of weakness.

5. This is one of several illustrations which have stuck with me for years but for which I can't trace the exact source; I have hence rewritten it, retaining the key concepts but using my own words.

4. <u>What Jesus has done</u>

1. Among many other examples, the work of N. T. Wright in this area has been very helpful.

2. Mahaney, C. J. (2006). *Living the cross-centred life.* Multnomah Books.

3. Adapted from: www.crossinglouisville.com/sermon/our-identity-in-christ/:

The Word of God says that in Jesus Christ...

I am the salt of the earth (Matt. 5:13)
I am a light of the world (Matt. 5:14)
I am God's child (Jn. 1:12)
I am promised eternal life (Jn. 6:47)
I am set free (Jn. 8:32; Rom. 8:2)
I am promised a full life (Jn. 10:10)
I am protected (Jn. 10:28)
I am His disciple (Jn. 13:15)
I have been chosen and God desires me to bear fruit (Jn. 15:1, 5)
I am Christ's friend (Jn. 15:15)
I am prayed for by Jesus Christ (Jn. 17:20-23)
I am united with other believers (Jn. 17:20-23)
I am a personal witness of Jesus Christ (Acts 1:8)

I am dead to sin (Rom. 1:12)
I have been justified (Rom. 5:1)
I am no longer condemned (Rom. 8:1-2)
I am assured all things work together for good (Rom. 8:28)
I am more than a conqueror (Rom. 8:37)
I am blameless (I Cor. 1:8)
I am in Him (1 Cor. 1:30; Eph. 1:7)
I possess the mind of Christ (I Cor. 2:16)
I am victorious (1 Cor. 15:57)
I am a holy temple (1 Cor. 6:19; Eph. 2:21)
I belong to God (1 Cor. 6:20)
I am a member of Christ's Body (1 Cor. 12:27)
I have been established, anointed and sealed by God (2 Cor. 1:21-22)
I am a new creation (2 Cor. 5:17)
I am a minister of reconciliation (2 Cor. 5:17-20)
I am the righteousness of God (2 Cor. 5:21)
I am God's coworker (2 Cor. 6:1)
I am crucified with Christ (Gal. 2:20)
I am redeemed from the curse of the Law (Gal. 3:13)
I am faithful (Eph. 1:1)
I am blessed in the heavenly realms with every spiritual blessing (Eph. 1:3)
I am chosen before the creation of the world (Eph. 1:4, 11)
I am holy and blameless (Eph. 1:4)
I am adopted as His child (Eph. 1:5)
I am given God's glorious grace lavishly and without restriction (Eph. 1:5, 8)
I have redemption (Eph. 1:8)
I am forgiven (Eph. 1:8; Col. 1:14)
I have purpose (Eph. 1:9; 3:11)
I have hope (Eph. 1:12)
I am included (Eph. 1:13)
I am sealed with the promised Holy Spirit (Eph. 1:13)
I am a saint (Eph. 1:18)
I am alive with Christ (Eph. 2:5)
I am raised up with Christ (Eph. 2:6; Col. 2:12)
I am seated with Christ in the heavenly realms (Eph. 2:6)
I have been shown the incomparable riches of God's grace (Eph. 2:7)
God has expressed His kindness to me (Eph. 2:7)
I am God's workmanship (Eph. 2:10)
I have been brought near to God through Christ's blood (Eph. 2:13)
I have peace (Eph. 2:14)
I have access to the Father (Eph. 2:18)

I am a member of God's household (Eph. 2:19)
I am secure (Eph. 2:20)
I am a dwelling for the Holy Spirit (Eph. 2:22)
I share in the promise of Christ Jesus (Eph. 3:6)
God's power works through me (Eph. 3:7)
I can approach God with freedom and confidence (Eph. 3:12)
I know there is a purpose for my sufferings (Eph. 3:13)
I can grasp how wide, long, high and deep Christ's love is (Eph. 3:18)
I am completed by God (Eph. 3:19)
I can bring glory to God (Eph. 3:21)
I have been called (Eph. 4:1; 2 Timothy 1:9)
I can be humble, gentle, patient and lovingly tolerant of others (Eph. 4:2)
I can mature spiritually (Eph. 4:15)
I can be certain of God's truths and the lifestyle which He has called me to (Eph. 4:17)
I can have a new attitude and a new lifestyle (Eph. 4:21-32)
I can be kind and compassionate to others (Eph. 4:32)
I can forgive others (Eph. 4:32)
I am a light to others, and can exhibit goodness, righteousness and truth (Eph. 5:8-9)
I can understand what God's will is (Eph. 5:17)
I can give thanks for everything (Eph. 5:20)
I don't have to always have my own agenda (Eph. 5:21)
I can honour God through marriage (Eph. 5:22-33)
I can parent my children with composure (Eph. 6:4)
I can be strong (Eph. 6:10)
I have God's power (Eph. 6:10)
I can stand firm in the day of evil (Eph. 6:13)
I am confident that God will perfect the work He has begun in me (Phil. 1:6)
I am persevering (Phil. 3:14)
I am a citizen of heaven (Phil. 3:20)
My heart and mind is protected with God's peace (Phil. 4:7)
I can do all things through Christ who strengthens me (Phil. 4:13)
I am not in want (Phil. 4:19)
I am qualified to share in His inheritance (Col. 1:12)
I am delivered (Col. 1:13)
I am growing (Col. 2:7)
I am hidden with Christ in God (Col. 3:3)
I am chosen and dearly loved (Col. 3:12)
I have not been given a spirit of fear, but of power, love and self-

discipline (2 Tim. 1:7)
I am not alone (Heb. 13:5)
I am born again (I Pet. 1:23)
I am healed from sin (I Pet. 2:24)
I am overcoming (I Jn. 4:4)
I am victorious (I Jn. 5:4)
I am born of God and the evil one cannot touch me (1 Jn. 5:18)
I am part of God's kingdom (Rev. 1:6)

4.   www.fathersloveletter.com/text.html (accessed 22/9/14).

5.   Lane, T. & Tripp, P. (2008). *How people change.* New Growth Press.

6.   I love this definition of forgiveness which I heard from Rikk Watts during a talk at the annual Northern Irish Christian gathering, New Horizon, on 26/7/13.

7.   We must keep in mind that 'cheap forgiveness' does no good to an unrepentant offender (particularly when the transgression has been serious) whose main need is to be confronted with his brokenness and challenged to find true salvation from sin and its effects.

8.   Benner, D. (1990). *Healing emotional wounds.* Baker Book House.

9.   Ted Williams' book, *Christ or therapy* (2010, The Wakeman Trust & Belmont House Publishing), has a chapter on this in relation to a critique on 'therapeutic forgiveness'.

5.   Power to change

1.   This is touching only briefly on a huge area and should not be read as a simplistic answer to the very real problem of anxiety. Anxiety disorders (including conditions such as generalised anxiety disorder, panic disorder, various phobias, obsessive-compulsive disorder and post-traumatic stress

disorder) can be some of the most distressing and disabling psychiatric conditions which may require comprehensive and intensive treatment by mental health professionals involving both medication and psychological therapy.

2. Hughes, S. (1986). *The Christian counsellor's pocket guide.* Kingsway.

3. Even TIME magazine felt this topic to be worthy of a recent cover story (www.mindful.org/mindfulness-practice/the-mindful-revolution).

4. Adapted from the very apt book title: Chester, T. (2010). *Captured by a better vision.* Inter-Varsity Press, where the writer presents how the extreme seduction of pornography needs to be overtaken by a deep realisation of the glory and beauty of Christ.

5. Ed Welch reminds us that in the midst of real struggle, desperate, trusting prayer from the heart can avail much: www.ccef.org/blog/spiritual-analysis-new-prayer-substitute.

6. Attributed to Ralph Waldo Emerson.

7. Bridges, J. (2012). *The transforming power of the gospel.* NavPress.

8. Tony Horsfall has written a helpful book on this topic: Horsfall, T. (2010). *Working from a place of rest: Jesus and the key to sustaining ministry.* BRF.

9. See, for example: Anderson, N. & Warner, T. (2000). *The beginner's guide to spiritual warfare.* Servant Publications; Murphy, E. (1996). *The handbook for spiritual warfare.* Thomas Nelson.

10. Bridges, J. (2012). *The transforming power of the gospel.* NavPress.

11. From: Ott, C. & Strauss, S. J. (2010). *Encountering theology of mission: Biblical foundations, historical developments, and contemporary issues.* Baker Academic (page 245).

12. www.bible.org/illustration/unmoved-rock (accessed 29/9/14).

6. <u>Eternal perspective</u>

1. For further study on these topics, it would be helpful to consult texts that present a balanced overview of the different biblical interpretations, for example: Grudem, W. (1994). *Systematic theology: An introduction to Biblical doctrine.* IVP; House, H. W. (1992). *Charts of Christian theology & doctrine.* Zondervan Publishing House.

2. A phrase from the introduction to that stirring song by the late Keith Green, 'I can't wait to get to heaven', sticks in my mind: *"...this is like living in a garbage can compared to what is going on up there".*

3. It is beyond the scope of this book to provide a fuller discussion of this complex and challenging subject.

   Readers are directed to some other helpful texts, such as: Yancey, P. (1997). *Where is God when it hurts?* Zondervan; Yancey, P. (1997). *Disappointment with God.* Zondervan; Martinez, P. (2007). *A thorn in the flesh.* IVP; Keller, T. (2013). *Walking with God through pain and suffering.* Dutton etc.

4. The book of Job is said to be the earliest book of the Bible; interesting to think how its message needs to be heard and known right at the start of our Christian journey.

5. www.watchgodwork.com/refined-like-silver (accessed 29/9/14).

7. <u>Our response</u>

1. Ortberg, J. (2014). *Soulkeeping*. Zondervan.

2. Some potentially useful further reading on this topic includes:

   - Eyre, S. (1995). *Time with God*. IVP.
   - Foster, R. (2008). *Celebration of discipline*. Hodder & Stoughton
   - McDonald, G. (2012). *Ordering your private world*. Thomas Nelson.
   - Ortberg, J. (2014). *Soulkeeping*. Zondervan.
   - Saxton, J. (2011). *Real God, real life*. Hodder & Stoughton.
   - Watson, D. (2014). *Discipleship*. Hodder Paperbacks.

3. Gary Smalley expands on this in his book: Smalley, G. (2004). *The DNA of relationships*. Tyndale.

4. The 'one anothering' passages provide a biblical basis for the godly relationships and practical care that can and should be the reality wherever the followers of Christ have gathered together. The following list has been taken from Nicewander, S. (2012). *Building a church counselling ministry (without killing the pastor)*. Day One (page 250):

   Love one another (Jn. 15:12, 17; 1 Thess. 3:12; 1 Jn. 3:11)
   Be kind to one another (Rom. 12:10a; Eph. 4:32)
   In honour give preference to one another (Rom. 12:10b; Phil. 2:3)
   Be like-minded (of the same mind) toward one another (Rom. 12:16; 15:5-6)
   Do not judge one another (Rom. 4:13)
   Edify one another (Rom. 14:19)
   Receive one another (Rom. 15:7)
   Admonish one another (Rom. 15:14)
   Minister to one another materially (Rom. 15:27)
   Greet one another (Rom. 16:16)
   Wait for one another (1 Cor. 11:33)
   Have the same care for one another (1 Cor. 12:25)
   Serve one another in love (Gal. 5:13)
   Beware lest you be consumed by one another (Gal. 5:15)

Do not provoke or envy one another (Gal. 5:26)
Bear one another's burdens (Gal. 6:2)
Bear with (forbear) one another in love (Eph. 4:2; Col. 3:13)
Forgive one another (Eph. 4:32)
Submit to one another (Eph. 5:21; 1 Pet. 5:5)
Do not lie to one another (Col. 3:9)
Comfort one another (1 Thess. 4:18; 5:11)
Consider one another (Heb. 10:24)
Do not speak evil of one another (Js. 4:11)
Do not grumble against one another (Js. 5:9)
Confess to one another (Js. 5:16)
Pray for one another (Js. 5:16)
Be hospitable to one another (1 Pet. 4:9)

C. The interface with mental health services

1. In this discussion, I am referring to mental health services as typically found within the government-funded National Health Service (NHS) of the UK.

2. I am using the term 'scientific psychology/psychiatry' to refer to the growing body of knowledge that has helped to define and treat mental disorders using approaches that have been robustly evaluated via scientific methods. It does imply 'secular' in that, generally speaking, these methods have not incorporated frameworks centred on the existence of a sovereign, personal supreme Being.

3. Adams, J. (1970). *Competent to counsel: Introduction to nouthetic counselling.* Zondervan.

4. The mission statement of CCEF is: *'Restoring Christ to counselling and counselling to the church'.* (www.ccef.org).

5. The BCC exists for the purpose of: *'Promoting personal change, centred on the Person of Christ, through the personal ministry of the Word'.* (www.biblicalcounselingcoalition.org).

6. *'For nearly 40 years, the ACBC (formerly known as NANC) has*

been certifying biblical counsellors to ensure doctrinal integrity and to promote excellence in biblical counselling' (www.biblicalcounseling.com).

7. The vision of BCUK is to promote: *'Christ-centred change, enabled by the Spirit, through the ministry of the Word, in the local church'* (www.biblicalcounselling.org.uk).

8. In the UK, this is usually done through the person's general practitioner (GP) unless in an emergency when crisis services can be activated.

9. Mike Emlet from CCEF has written a helpful article about psychiatric medication from a Christian perspective: Emlet, M. R. (2012). *Listening to Prozac...and to the Scriptures: A primer on psychoactive medications.* The Journal of Biblical Counseling, 26 (1), 11-22.

10. A helpful critique of secular psychologies and a Christian response can be found in: Hurding, R. F. (2003). *Roots & shoots: A guide to counselling and psychotherapy (updated edition).* Hodder & Stoughton. For a more in-depth look at the interface between Christianity and psychology, readers may consult: Johnson, E. L. (Ed.) 2010. *Psychology & Christianity: Five Views.* IVP Academic.

Further resources

There is an abundance of good resources on this and related topics; this is a non-exhaustive list of potentially useful references and resources for further study and help:

Books that help us better understand the gospel

These books help to describe the gospel of grace in all its richness and majesty:

Hession, R. (1950). *The Calvary road.* Christian Literature Crusade.

Chandler, M. (2012). *The explicit gospel.* IVP.

Piper, J. (2005). *God is the gospel: Meditations on God's love as the gift of Himself.* IVP.

Kraft, A. (2008). *Good news for those trying harder.* David C. Cook.

Tchividjian, T. (2011). *Jesus + nothing = everything.* Crossway.

Mahaney, C. J. (2006). *Living the cross centred life.* Multnomah Books.

Edwards, G. (1992). *The secret of the Christian life.* Tyndale House.

Greear, J. D. (2013). *Stop asking Jesus into your heart: How to know for sure you are saved.* Broadman & Holman.

Bridges, J. (2012). *The transforming power of the gospel.* NavPress.

Edman, V. R. (1984). *They found the secret.* Zondervan.

Bible-based, gospel-centred counselling approaches

These books describe an approach that seeks to apply the Bible/gospel openly and directly to people's problems in living:

Nicewander, S. (2012). *Building a church counselling ministry (without killing the pastor): A collaborative model for local churches, pastors, and biblical counsellors.* Day One.

MacDonald, J., Kellemen, B., Viars, S. (2013). *Christ-centred biblical counselling.* Harvest House.

Hedges, B. G. (2010). *Christ formed in you: The power of the gospel for personal change.* Shepherd Press.

Adams, J. (1970). *Competent to counsel: Introduction to nouthetic counselling.* Zondervan.

MacArthur, J. & Master's College Faculty. (2005). *Counselling: How to counsel biblically.* Thomas Nelson.

Kellemen, B. (2014). *Gospel-centred counselling: How Christ changes lives.* Zondervan.

Lane, T. & Tripp, P. (2009). *How people change.* New Growth Press.

Tripp, P. (2002). *Instruments in the Redeemer's hands.* P & R Publishing Company.

Kellemen, B. (2014). *Scripture and counselling: God's Word for life in a broken world.* Zondervan.

Powlison, D. (2003). *Seeing with new eyes.* P & R Publishing Company.

Powlison, D. (2005). *Speaking the truth in love.* New Growth Press.

Chester, T. (2008). *You can change.* IVP.